SOS:

Strategies for Online Survival

The essential getting-started guide for virtual teachers

Desiré Mosser

Copyright © 2020 by Desiré Mosser

All rights reserved. No part of this publication may be reproduced, distributed, or transmitted in any form or by any means, including photocopying, recording, or other electronic or mechanical methods, without the prior written permission of the publisher, author or copyright holder, except in the case of brief quotations embodied in critical reviews and certain other noncommercial uses permitted by copyright law.

All information contained in this book is subject to change.

Dedicated to the hardworking teachers who do whatever it takes to guide their students to success!

TABLE OF CONTENTS

Foreword   11

Introduction   13
   Brick-and-Mortar versus Virtual   14
   Something to Look Forward To   15
   Using This Book   17
   Before Getting Started: Self-Reflection   19

WTF: Winning The Fight Against First-Day Frustration   21
   Get Organized   23
      Schedule for Success   23
      Folders for Sanity   23
   Managing Email Workflow Boundaries   26
      Setting Email Communication Expectations   27
      If You Have Nothing Nice to Email ...   28
      Minimizing Email Disturbances   28
   Managing Phone Workflow Boundaries   29
      Setting Phone Expectations   29
      After Controlling Yourself, Control Your Phone   30
   Practicing Self-Care   32
      Be Kind to Yourself   32
      Move Your Body   33
      Choose Healthy Snacks   34
      Do What You Enjoy   34
      Get Your Z's   34
   Secrets of Success   36
   Taking Action   36

MVP: Managing a Virtual Platform   39
   Course Announcement Page   39

Developing Social Presence	39
Mapping Out Your Curriculum	41
Welcoming Your Students to Class	42
Welcome Email	42
Example Welcome Email	44
Office Hours	45
Appointments	45
Possible Appointment Types	46
Welcome Call	46
Monthly Check-In	47
One-On-One Academic Assistance	47
Exam Review Sessions	47
Appointment Quick Tips	47
Remembering the Phone Shy	49
Secrets of Success	50
Taking Action	51
BRB: Building Relationships, BABY!	**53**
Revisiting the Course Announcement Page	54
Course Announcement Page Best Practices	54
Welcome Calls: The Golden Egg	56
Connecting through Phone Calls	58
Playing Cat and Mouse	59
Bonding with Students through Email	60
Supporting ELL students	62
Building Classroom Community	64
Building Teacher/Parent Relationships	67
Staying Connected with Coworkers	69
Curbing Your Negativity	71
Secrets of Success	72

Taking Action	73
CSI: Customer Service Integration	**75**
Watch Your Tone: Email Etiquette	75
Learn to Walk Away	77
Assume Others Have the Best Intentions	80
Secrets of Success	81
Taking Action	82
LMAO: Leading Meetings All Online	**83**
Quick Online Meeting Tips	83
Challenges of Online Meetings	86
Prepping Student Meetings and Live Lessons	90
Scheduling	91
Online Meeting and Live Lesson Tech Prep	92
Practice Your Tech	93
One Starfish at a Time	95
Secrets of Success	97
Taking Action	98
LLC: Live-Lesson Creation	**101**
Determining the Length of Your Live Lesson	101
Limiting Student Attendance	102
Live-Lesson Planning	102
Preplanning	103
Create a Learning Goal	103
Activate Prior Knowledge	103
Plan Content Delivery	103
Time for Engagement	104
Check for Understanding	105
Follow-Up	105

Getting the Word Out	106
Starting the Lesson	107
Engage, Don't Lecture	109
Handling Disruption and Behavior Issues	112
After the Meeting	112
Secrets of Success	113
Taking Action	114

TGIF: Teaching and Guiding with Intentional Feedback 117

Providing STARR Feedback	118
Providing Timely Feedback	120
Feed Forward	120
Efficiency Tips	121
Save Your Grading/Feedback Notes	122
Group Grading	124
Late Work and Cheating	124
Late Work	124
Cheating … Oh No You Didn't!	125
Secrets of Success	129
Taking Action	130

TMI: Time Management Ideas 133

Right On Schedule	133
Allowing for Flexibility	134
Schedule Time for You	137
Schedule Examples	137
Chunking Schedule	138
Hourly Schedule	138
Daily Check-Off Schedule	139
Making Time for Professional Development	139
Secrets of Success	140

Taking Action	141
BFF: Balancing Function and Family	**143**
They Don't Always Get It	144
Lord of the Phones	145
The Family Team	147
Remember, It Gets Better!	151
Secrets of Success	152
Taking Action	152
Conclusion	**155**
Resources	**159**
Lesson Planning Sheet	159
Live-Lesson Checklists	161
About the Author	**167**

Foreword

If you're lucky, professionally speaking, you'll spend at least one chapter of your career working with talented professionals who are at the top of their field. Their expertise in practicing their craft will provide you with the opportunity to improve your own practice, while offering you encouragement and challenging you to learn and grow.

The very best professional environments foster collaboration, risk taking, and honesty. You'll find people working together to try new ideas, reflecting on their performance and sharing resources to ensure that the team or organization remains committed to its core values through growth. These high-performing teams draw other talented people in by shining their enthusiasm and positive examples like a beacon.

But if you're very lucky, these talented members of your team will also become friends. And through their friendship, they'll hold you accountable to your team and to yourself. It's because I've been fortunate to develop just such a friendship with Desiré Mosser that I'm thrilled to provide this introduction to her book, as well as to her heart.

Desiré and I met, strangely enough, while working for rival virtual schools. Through our interactions online, I could see that she was committed to helping other online teachers with practical advice and humor. Her sincere desire to mentor online teachers from any virtual school led her to develop social media groups that encouraged honest conversations around challenges and best practices. She helped to elevate the collaboration and camaraderie for online teachers throughout the state of Florida.

And when I had the opportunity to hire Desiré, I didn't hesitate. Her passion for coaching teachers toward a more student-centered way of work is contagious. Her passion comes through in her writing, and it will inspire you too.

In her humorous and relatable book, Desiré will increase your understanding of the most powerful ways teachers can connect to build strong relationships with colleagues and students. She covers topics such as motivating kids to work, best practices for online meetings, handling the sometimes-tricky world of online communication and feedback, and even balancing family with a work-from-home career.

The Pasco eSchool faculty, and the entire Pasco County School district, have leaned on her advice and expertise throughout the expansion of our virtual instruction program and as we continued teaching during the COVID-19 pandemic. I know you'll enjoy this journey of discovery and reflection as you build your skill set. I'm better for having Desiré as a colleague and friend, and I'm confident the time spent with this book will lead you to have a newfound respect for the craft of virtual instruction.

Virtual smiles,

JoAnne M. Glenn
Principal
Pasco eSchool
Spring Hill, FL

Introduction

> *"Everyone knows teaching online is a breeze. Time to catch up on some daytime TV!"*

Before you start this book, take a look at the statement above. If that's something you've thought, then you might want to start working on a plan B.

I don't want to sugarcoat this for you. If you're just now starting out on this adventure and not too heavily invested, it is a great time to change your plans and do something else.

It's common to think that online teaching is a piece of cake. Maybe you even heard that from a friend or someone's social media post. Maybe you believe the rumors that when you teach online, you'll get to stay at home, watch TV, go to the mall, keep your house spotless, and so on. Maybe you've read that online teachers don't work much and lesson planning is a thing of the past. Let's get clear on this now: none of those things are true.

The reality is, I work more now than I ever did as a classroom teacher. When you teach online, there are days when you'll forget to eat, forget what your family looks like, and forget that your body needs to move so that you don't develop blood clots. For the first few months of your new journey, you may even find yourself staring at your bloodshot eyes in the mirror, asking, "What have I done?"

Are you still here? Good. Then you just might have what it takes to teach online.

Brick-and-Mortar versus Virtual

If you're new to teaching online, much of what you're accustomed to in a brick-and-mortar setting will look and feel different. You will have moments reminiscent of your first year of teaching all over again. You may experience bouts of uncertainty, apprehension, and insecurity. Other times, you may feel like you won the lotto and rule the world.

As an online teacher, you're embarking on a new journey filled with unexpected surprises along the way. I'm not joking when I say it's more work, but there are important benefits. I've been teaching for more than twenty-four years. After nine years teaching kids from preschool to grade 8, I moved to online education. For the past fifteen years, I've taught science and leadership skills, and served as an instructional coach for more than 100 online teachers. I've seen both sides, taught in both worlds.

While this book is going to confront some of the challenges you're in for, it's also going to discuss some of the benefits. But these benefits don't come on their own. You have to work hard to create a routine—and stick to it. That is your key to controlling your time and keeping your sanity.

Once I found a routine, I was able to manage my time effectively, gain more flexibility within my workday, and finally stop frequently feeling overwhelmed and faced with constant pressure during a typical school year. Essentially, I became more effective working at my own pace. It took me twenty-one years to get there, but I don't want you enduring the same long wait. That's why I'm sharing all (okay, most) of my secrets with you so you can get there even sooner.

Something to Look Forward To

The past year has thrown a lot of new teachers toward a virtual path. During the 2017-2018 school year, more than 297,000 students were enrolled in 501 full-time virtual schools across the United States, while blended schools numbered 300 with more than 132,000 enrolled students.[1] Based on the average number of students per teacher in these virtual and blended classrooms, we can assume there were upwards of 10,000 teachers teaching virtually in the 2017-2018 school year.[2] That's an impressive number, for sure, but it was completely dwarfed in the 2019-2020 school year.

By March 2020, thanks to COVID-19, 104,000 US brick-and-mortar schools had closed, leaving 47.9 million students and more than three million teachers thrown into the virtual school trenches, far too many without training or proper support.[3,4] After countless Zoom meetings organized through the online teaching Facebook support page, The Virtual Balcony, and within my school's district, I found these reluctant virtual teachers faced tremendous hurdles, but they also saw the benefits that could come from teaching online, once they got the hang of it.

What are these benefits? I'm biased, so let's look at what some other people have to say. Over 100,000 new online teachers were polled on Facebook and asked what

---

[1] http://nepc.colorado.edu/sites/default/files/publications/Virtual%20Schools%202019.pdf
[2] http://blogs.edweek.org/edweek/DigitalEducation/2019/05/growth_of_online_schools_slowing.html
[3] https://www.brookings.edu/blog/the-avenue/2020/03/20/as-classes-move-online-during-covid-19-what-are-disconnected-students-to-do/
[4] https://learningpolicyinstitute.org/blog/impact-covid-19-recession-teaching-positions

some of the best parts of teaching online were. Here are a handful of their responses. Be warned; some of them might stun you:

- Building stronger relationships with colleagues
- Better communication with my students' parents
- Opportunities to connect with my students one-on-one without an entire class seeking attention
- The ability to use the restroom whenever I want
- Learning about new technology that I can use to enhance student learning
- Finding new ways to be creative and innovative in my virtual classroom
- No commute time
- Wearing elastic-waist pants on a daily basis with fuzzy socks
- Not having to deal with student behavior issues

It comes as no surprise that the thrill of at-will restroom use made it to the list but were you shocked to see things like building stronger relationships, better communication with parents, and connecting with students? It's true. Between the flexibility in your schedule and your ability to really dig in one-on-one, virtual teaching creates a far more fertile environment for communication and relationship building with parents, students, and colleagues.

For educators who want to see the impact they make on a student-by-student basis, virtual teaching is a dream come true. And on top of that, it's easier to plan curriculum, provide students with meaningful feedback, and enjoy the students when you don't have to deal with the day-to-day stresses, demands, and challenging behaviors in the classroom.

Using This Book

This book is broken down into nine sections to make jumping around easier. That way, you can deal with those topics you are struggling with the most first. We're going to start our journey jumping right into the steps you need to take to get your first day under control. Next, we'll cover how to manage your virtual platform. After that, we'll cover building relationships with parents, students, and colleagues and then move on to customer service integration. Our next topics will be leading online meetings and the heart of the book, live lesson creation.

Once that's complete, we'll cover intentional feedback and time-management ideas. I'll close out the book with a discussion of balancing your online teaching/work-from-home career with having a family.

In each section, you also will find checklists, action steps, and reflection exercises to help you learn how to integrate the lessons into your teaching practice. Each chapter contains tips and tricks that have proven effective over more than fifteen years by online teachers from around the US, and many have a focus on social emotional learning (SEL) standards.

In the Resources section, you'll find templates and other resources you can use to integrate the tips in this book with your day-to-day teaching.

> **Social Emotional Learning (SEL)**
>
> Most of us are born with the capacity to feel emotions but learning to manage emotions properly as a means to setting and achieving goals, having empathy, making good decisions, and creating and maintaining positive relationships isn't always innate. Instead, it's up to us to help our students develop social emotional learning that leads them to becoming positive, functional, empathetic adults. As we move through this work, the best practices and suggestions provided keep our students' SEL at the forefront of what we do as virtual teachers.

As educators, we are rarely given the time to reflect on our teaching practices unless we purposefully make the time to do so. I encourage you to take the time, while working through this book, to engage in the reflection activities so that you may use this as an opportunity to learn and grow as an educator.

Make this book yours—put your mark on it by underlining, highlighting, circling, making notes, marking pages, and treating this book as an interactive tool while you move into the world of distance learning.

And if you do all that with an adult beverage in hand, I won't say anything.

Before Getting Started: Self-Reflection

Take a moment to think about distance learning. What are two questions that come to mind when you think about teaching students online?

_____

_____

_____

_____

What is something you hope to gain by reading this book?

_____

_____

_____

_____

What is something you are excited about when it comes to teaching online?

_____

_____

_____

_____

What is something you are apprehensive/fearful about when it comes to teaching online?

_____

_____

_____

_____

What are some pros and cons you expect to encounter as you begin teaching online?

Pros:

_____

_____

_____

_____

Cons:

_____

_____

_____

_____

WTF: Winning The Fight Against First-Day Frustration

"Where do I even start?"
You start with today, and you go one day at a time.

No matter how long you've wanted to become a virtual teacher, getting started has its challenges. I'd be lying if I said this career would never feel overwhelming or just plain impossible at times when first starting off. Heck, I'd be lying if I told you that moments of frustration and feeling overwhelmed don't pop in from time to time even after you've been teaching online for a while. It comes and goes ... much like my time spent at the gym.

You'll notice that the work goes really smoothly for a while, and you'll feel like you have things figured out. You'll be in full-on beast mode ... and then, BAM, you'll find yourself so overwhelmed and stressed, you'll be shoving a gallon of rocky road ice cream down your gullet, wondering if you can survive the pay cut that would come with working at Starbucks.

This is a universal truth, and here's why: think about all the things you're accustomed to doing in a traditional brick-and-mortar classroom each day.

- Lesson planning
- Presenting new material
- Conquering classroom management
- Answering 300 questions, 50 being the same one asked over and over again
- Navigating small-group instruction
- Creating student-friendly resources

- Scaffolding information based on level
- Paperwork ... lots and lots of paperwork
- Monitoring individual student growth
- Parent/teacher conferences

Really, I could fill a book with this stuff—the list here is just a small percentage of what you do in a day. And it doesn't include all the other "stuff" that comes with being a teacher, like car line, lunch duty, hall duty, bathroom duty, duty to make sure others are on duty—the list goes on and on.

A few of these tasks are removed once you begin teaching virtually, but there are more than enough new tasks to fill the time. As a virtual teacher, you now need to add in an extremely high volume of emails, phone calls, online meetings, live lessons, individualized academic assistance, text messages, and the occasional late-night call from a panicked student regarding an assignment that's due at midnight.

Although the distance-learning setting looks and feels different, the ongoing list of tasks is just as long, if not longer. On top of all that, now that you're working from the comfort of your home, your work will always be with you.

In order to conquer the distance-learning world and develop into a successful, efficient, and effective online teacher, it's important to understand some of the best practices of online teaching and the reasons behind them. With the right know-how, you'll be rocking the online world in no time.

Get Organized

You might be wondering how you can get organized for a position you haven't really started or how to reorganize yourself midstream if the school year is underway and you feel like you're drowning. Believe it or not, there are two things you can do right now that will set you up for success or get you back on track if things haven't gone the way you would like so far.

Schedule for Success

A schedule will be your key to success. Throughout the book, I'll cover the finer points of scheduling, notably in the Time Management Ideas (TMI) section, but for now, just think about what hours you'll be available to work without interruption. And remember, you don't have to work eight consecutive hours. If you can grab two hours four times throughout the day, that works too.

You have flexibility throughout your day, which will feel very different from what you may be accustomed to in a traditional setting. There won't be a bell ringing to alert you to stop what you're doing and move on to the next activity. You are *powerful*! You are now in charge of your own schedule and can make it work to fit the needs of your students as well as your own.

Folders for Sanity

So much information comes your way in the first few weeks. You'll probably be blasted with an overwhelming number of documents, such as manuals, how-tos, shared documents from friendly coworkers, training materials, and district information. With all this information coming in, you can easily find yourself misplacing items or, since you just don't know what you don't know, you might have no idea how (or if) the documents will be helpful later.

Rather than designate your email the lost grave of misunderstood documents, create a folder system that makes everything relatively easy to locate when you discover a need for it. You will end up personalizing this system based on your work style, but to get started, create these six folders:

- *District info*: Each time you receive something from the district, put it into this file. Then, if something comes up and you realize you actually need information from one of those emails, you can go back and dig it out.

- *Things to do in the next two weeks*: This folder ensures that important tasks don't fall through the cracks and that to-do emails don't get buried in the pile of 100 other emails you get throughout the day.

> Add a category in your schedule for browsing the *Things to do* folder and a check-off line to ensure you don't overlook a task.

- *I don't know*: An *I don't know* folder is a great way to categorize items that you have no idea what to do with. Tuck those aside and ask your coach or mentor teacher when you have the opportunity to help clarify what you need to do with those items.

- *Course-specific info*: This folder holds the resources you get that help support you and your students in the course you're teaching. This may include answer keys, enrichment activities, sample collaboration assignments, and resources to enhance the curriculum. Often, your fellow teachers will want to share what they have to help make your life easier. You may not fully understand what you have until it comes time to use it, so put them in this folder for safekeeping and easy access.

- *Passwords*: Throughout each day, you'll be logging into many websites that require a username and password. Trust me when I say that you never, ever, ever want to rely only on your laptop to remember these passwords and usernames—because eventually, you will get a new laptop, and figuring out all these logins will be a nightmare. Instead, keep a secure paper file with all that information.

- *KUDOS*: Of all the folders you create, the *KUDOS* file is the most important. In this folder, you'll stick all those emails that come your way that tell you what a badass you are and what a fantastic job you're doing with your students. Stack that file full! There will be days when you ask yourself why you even bother working so hard. You'll blame yourself for students who choose not to do their work in class. You'll hold their lack of motivation on your shoulders. During those times where you're feeling frustrated and overwhelmed, it's important to open your *KUDOS* file and remind yourself of all the great things that have happened and

ARE happening. Remind yourself that what you're doing DOES make a difference; remember that we all have bad days and you will get through it.

Managing Email Workflow Boundaries

As you probably expect, email is a primary communication tool for virtual teachers. School administrators, fellow teachers, students, parents, vendors, and others will all use email to reach out to you, ensuring you're bombarded with emails seven days a week, at all hours of the night. Sometimes, not responding to emails within a nine-second time frame will result in even more emails rushing in.

Even when it seems the sneaky emails are procreating in your inbox, you must remember that they are a lifeline of communication for your students and their parents. Over the years, I've gotten emails from students about deaths in the family, from parents who don't understand why their kids are failing, and my favorite of all, students reaching out to thank me for being there for them—for listening to them and for caring.

Also, the longer you do this, the more you'll realize that receiving emails from students, no matter when they might land in your inbox, means they are trying to engage in their learning. It's when you stop receiving emails that you should be worried. Welcome those emails with open arms and be thankful they are trying.

Finally, while you can't control what emails come in, you can control how you respond to them. While the paragraphs above are good to remember because they help you maintain compassion as you look at 9,999 new emails each day, understanding that you can control your response to emails is the point that will help you maintain your sanity. Unwritten rule #7845 of online teaching states:

One shall admit that while they cannot control incoming emails, they can, and will, control their responses.

Setting Email Communication Expectations

Our reactions to other people teach them what they can expect from us. This includes your reaction to emails. If you start off answering emails on weekends, people will expect that from you in the future. For some students and parents, Sunday at 11 p.m. is the only time they will have time or access to their online schooling. Work schedules, family situations, homelessness, and other challenges can affect a student's workflow.

One of the benefits of teaching online is that we have more flexibility to meet the needs of our students; however, we have to be mindful of the precedent we set. If you don't feel comfortable responding to a text at 11 p.m., you shouldn't. It's also not necessary to respond to all emails on the same day they were received. Set boundaries for yourself and stick with them. Most often, it's a lack of boundaries that makes our days overwhelming.

It's also important to make sure you're modeling behavior that you want your students to exercise. If you don't want to encourage students to email you at 11 p.m. on a Saturday night, make sure you don't send emails to them at that hour, on Saturday. You have to train your kiddos to follow your communication expectations; modeling those expectations yourself is a good place to start.

Likewise, if you set a robocall or text to all your students on a Friday night at 7 p.m., you can't really get upset when they start responding an hour later.

If You Have Nothing Nice to Email ...

The last thing we want to do is give students a reason to stop engaging. When you get an email that upsets you or an outside situation has you feeling upset, take a break rather than responding to an email. This is something I cover in much more detail in the Customer Service Integration (CSI) chapter.

When students email over the weekend, or at other times when it's inconvenient to answer, simply respond during your normal working hours by saying, "Good morning! I received your email from this weekend and just wanted to check in to see how I can help. Please let me know when you have time. I look forward to connecting with you soon."

Minimizing Email Disturbances

Depending on what program you use, your email may be able to send an automatic message once you've placed it on Do Not Disturb or Out of the Office. If so, you can create a message that tells emailers you are away from your desk and will respond to their message when you return. This should help reduce instances of multiple contact attempts when you don't immediately respond to an email.

Even when you're working, it's annoying and inefficient to be pulled from other tasks every time the email alert chimes from your inbox. A University of California study found that it takes an average of 23 minutes, 15 seconds to get yourself back on track after being interrupted.[5] This means that even if you're lucky enough to get distracted only a few times a day, you lose an hour of work! Turn that sound off so you don't hear emails coming in and feel the anxiety rise when you can't get to them immediately.

Managing Phone Workflow Boundaries

Email isn't the only form of communication you need to have boundaries around. Some days, you will wonder if the phone ever stops ringing. Depending on the number of students you have, your phone may ring more often than Amazon delivering random impulse buys to my front door. It may also ring more during certain times of the year, such as when you have deadlines in place and students are required to complete an online course by a certain time. The three to four weeks leading up to the deadline can get a little out of control. Those students who have dragged their feet, despite you nudging them along, will suddenly pick up the pace and decide that the time to complete all of their work is NOW!

Last-minute communication attempts can be anxiety inducing for everyone involved. This can, in turn, ramp up the number of phone calls you receive on your end. The good news is, there are ways to control and manage incoming calls.

Setting Phone Expectations

When you're required to reach out to your students by phone, clarify any misconceptions they might have when it comes to

---

[5]https://affect.media.mit.edu/pdfs/16.Mark-CHI_Email.pdf

your availability. This is a great time to review your weekly office hours and communication expectations.

Speaking of office hours, be sure to keep yours posted on the front page of your course and consistently remind students of them in emails and conversations. You can also add the information to the signature in your email so every email to both parents and students contains an easily accessible reminder.

One of the issues virtual teachers face with phone calls is that they imply a certain urgency to your communications. But remember, you do NOT have to respond to every phone call on the same day you receive it. Not everything in life has an immediate turnaround, and it's okay to help kids learn this life lesson. Sometimes there's a lag, and that's okay. Trust me, there are no math emergencies, no matter what others might tell you.

The important piece is to return a call within a reasonable amount of time. What "reasonable" means to you is often determined by your district. In my experience, this is generally within twenty-four hours, not including weekends.

Finally, make sure you don't give your personal cell number to students. Help yourself further distinguish your personal life from your professional life and see if your school will provide you with a designated number for your work-related business. Google Voice is also a good option.

After Controlling Yourself, Control Your Phone

Your phone isn't just an instrument of torture. It also offers tools that can help you better manage incoming calls at any time of day. One of the most vital of these tools is the Do Not Disturb function, which you should enable at the end of your workday. This will send your callers directly to voicemail so you can take time for yourself and respond to them in the morning.

If your district pays for a line for you through a vendor such as Dialpad, oftentimes you can even set up an automatic text to be sent back to students if they call or text during your Do Not Disturb hours. Many online tools, such as Google Voice, have a Do Not Disturb option, allowing you to set manually the hours you would like your calls to be automatically sent to voicemail.

When I was new to teaching online, one night I'd forgotten to put my phone to Do Not Disturb. My school line rang at 11 p.m. while my three-year-old and newborn were sleeping. If the ringing had woken either of them, heads would have rolled. Any new parent can relate to the rage that builds when your bedtime-routine planning is ruined by a ringing phone. It didn't, however, so instead of rage, I felt worry.

With any late-night phone call, I immediately thought something bad had happened to someone, so I answered, my sleepy voice sounding groggy, raspy, and somewhat confused. "Hello, this is Mrs. Mosser, may I ask who is calling and if everything is okay?" The student on the other end of the line, put off by my obviously sleepy voice, told me he didn't mean to call, he must have dialed the wrong number.

I wanted to teach this sweet cherub a life lesson that calling someone other than your best friend or parents at eleven o'clock at night is not acceptable. Rather than shouting, "And the Emmy goes to …," I decided to tell him that when I heard my work phone ringing at that late hour, it woke me up and made me think something was terribly wrong, so I just had to answer. This wasn't entirely true but made it so much more dramatic. Turns out the student just needed me to reset an assignment for him, and this was the only hour he could find time to work on it. Being the softy that I am, I reset that student assignment after we hung up and saw it in my inbox ready for grading the very next day.

Another thing you can do is turn off your ringer. When you're not working, are in a meeting, grading student work, planning a lesson, or taking a break, turn off the ringer on your phone so calls roll automatically to voicemail.

Lastly, consider changing the chime of your work-line ringer. Find yourself feeling anxious each time you hear the chime of your phone? Hearing the same ring sound day after day can get annoying and can also cause anxiety over time. Choose something upbeat and cheerful and switch the jingle from time to time!

Practicing Self-Care

From day one, you need to establish self-care strategies to ensure that you keep your sanity in what can be a busy world. Teachers often take care of everyone else and forget to take care of themselves.

Be Kind to Yourself

Part of being kind to yourself on this wild ride is recognizing that you will make a lot of mistakes along the way. I know this will be hard for some of our type-A teacher personalities—you know who you are! I'm one myself. However, making mistakes is a sign that you're trying something new. If you aren't making mistakes, then you aren't trying new things, and you aren't growing and developing as an online educator.

Embracing a growth mindset when learning a new skill is an important part of the process. It allows you to make a mistake, learn from it, and move forward. Don't obsess on the fact that you made an error and get yourself worked up over it. To grow and develop a stronger online educator skill set, we have to be fearless in our teaching. Being fearful of making mistakes or not knowing how to do something leads to educator stagnation.

Don't become frozen in your fear, unable to move forward, unable to try new things, unable to innovate, unable to grow and develop your online teaching skills. Ask questions of others and be a fearless teacher!

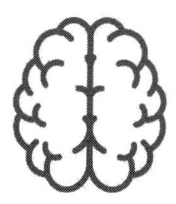

> "Mistakes are so interesting. Here's a wonderful mistake. Let's see what we can learn from it."
>
> — Carol S. Dweck, *Scientific American*, "The Secret to Raising Smart Kids"

Move Your Body

There will be days where you'll find yourself sitting in front of your computer for hours on end. You might even start making grunting noises when standing or begin complaining about aches and pains at the end of the workday. Much of this can be a side effect of sitting for too long in one position. It's important to get up and move around throughout the day to cut down on these aches and pains and also to decompress and rest our amazing brains.

- Sit on a yoga ball for better posture.
- Invest in a walking treadmill or standing desk.
- Set a time to stretch every hour.
- Go outside and take a short walk.

- Invest in a pair of Bluetooth headphones so you can walk around while talking to students.
- Go for a bike ride with family members.

Choose Healthy Snacks

Grazing is not something that just happens on the plains of Wyoming. Mindless eating is an uphill battle for many of us who teach online. Finish a call, get a snack. Grade fifty papers, reward yourself with a snack. Cleared out your email inbox? Why, you deserve a snack! Didn't respond to that nastygram the way you would have liked to? You deserve a BIG snack! When grazing and rewarding yourself with tasty treats, it's important to have healthy choices on hand. Are you familiar with the Freshman 15? Whelp, there's also the Online Teacher 20. Beware!

Do What You Enjoy

You know all those things you like doing in your free time? Spending time with your family, DIY crafts, yard work, exercise, reading, sports, napping, etc.? It's critical that you make the time to engage in all the things that fill your bucket. Teacher burnout is a real thing and often results from not taking part in the things you enjoy most in life. Resentment sets in, and it's exhausting to try to find the spark for activities for which you once had a passion. Be intentional about scheduling time each day to take part in the things that inspire you!

Get Your Z's

An important component of self-care is ensuring you give your body time to rest and recharge. Without proper rest, you'll be running on an empty tank. You could even have trouble with problem solving, controlling emotions, and coping with change—all skills that online teachers need in spades![6] This can make it difficult to focus, meet job expectations, effectively communicate with those around you, and can result in the loss of patience for others.

One way to help ensure you get enough sleep is to invest in a pair of blue-blocking glasses. Blue blockers help in reducing exposure to blue light waves that can keep you awake at night. Side note: nobody ever said that you can't take a midafternoon siesta on a slow day! BONUS!

SELF-CARE

- Be kind to yourself.
- Try new things.
- Make mistakes.
- Teach fearlessly.
- Grow as a professional.
- Move your body.
- Choose healthy snacks.
- Do what you enjoy.
- Get your z's.

---

[6]https://www.nhlbi.nih.gov/health-topics/sleep-deprivation-and-deficiency

Secrets of Success

- Take one day at a time.

- Use Do Not Disturb for email, phone calls, and text messages on your phone and computer.

- Learn from your mistakes and move forward from them.

- Ask questions and teach without fear of failure.

- Practice having a growth mindset.

- Embrace self-care strategies.

Taking Action

This week, to get myself organized for teaching online, I will

_____

_____

_____

_____

When I don't remember how to do something in my virtual classroom, I will

_____

_____

_____

_____

Making mistakes at work tends to make me feel

_____

_____

_____

_____

Moving forward, when making mistakes, I will remember that

_____

_____

_____

_____

Two strategies of self-care that I will incorporate into my workday, starting today, are

_____

_____

_____

_____

MVP: Managing a Virtual Platform

"Wipe your feet!"
Get your virtual platform ready for visitors.

Before we can invite students into our virtual classrooms, we need to get it prepared for visitors. Dust off the lessons, vacuum under the virtual couch, put fresh flowers in the online vases. So, what are we waiting for? Let's do this!

Course Announcement Page

Your course announcement page or homepage is the first thing students will see when they enter their online classroom. Depending on the Learning Management System (LMS), or the platform your school or district has chosen for distance learning, you may or may not have the ability to update and make changes to this area. For the purposes of this book, let's assume you'll have some ability to adjust your course announcement page.

Now, let's go over some best practices for using this area.

Developing Social Presence

Your announcement page is an opportunity to build social presence within your virtual classroom. Think of it like your online bulletin board, similar to those you may have decorated while working in a brick-and-mortar setting. Remember those days of stapling borders to colorful butcher-block paper? Well, now you get to skip the staples and decorate an online page your students will see first thing when they log in.

> "Social presence is defined as the ability of participants in a community to project themselves, socially and emotionally, as real people through a medium of communication." (Garrison and Anderson (2003), E-learning in the 21st Century: A Framework for Research and Practice)
>
> "In virtual environments, social presence is generally described as a feeling of group participation and belonging associated with multiple users of a virtual environment." (Franceschi, Katherine & Lee, Ronald & Zanakis, Stelios & Hinds, David. (2009). Engaging Group E-Learning in Virtual Worlds. J. of Management Information Systems. 26. 73-100. 10.2753/MIS0742-1222260104.)

Your announcement page is an opportunity to personalize your classroom and give students a glimpse into who you are as a real person, provide your students with a sense of belonging, and start building your virtual relationships. Essentially, it's that first impression everyone says is so important. Your goal should be to use the page to help your students feel welcomed, comfortable, and excited about what lies ahead for them in their online course!

In the "Building Relationships, BABY! (BRB)" section, I discuss some ways you can use the announcement page to build relationships with students. But when you're first starting out, share some of the following information to start creating rapport:

- Name of the course
- Photo of you, your family, and your pets
- Favorite student-appropriate shows and songs
- Phone/text number to reach you
- Office hours
- Link to your appointment scheduler
- Additional resources for student use
- Posted meeting times, upcoming events, school activities

Mapping Out Your Curriculum

If you're creating your own lessons and/or activities for students to engage in, there are a few things to keep in mind to avoid totally overwhelming yourself during the week.

First, take into account the number of students you will have in your course, and create lessons that cut out the fluff and access learning as efficiently as possible. If you assign 100 online learners an assignment each day of the week and require each of those assignments to be submitted for grading by you each day, you have set yourself up for grading 500 assignments in one week. That does not account for the time you will need to answer emails, provide possible online office hours, return phone calls, attend required school-related meetings, and so on.

Next, you want to spread your assignments apart. Possibly create a self-check activity that is autograded for one to two assignments throughout the week. When assigning larger projects where students may need to create an end project, provide them with several days to complete the assignment. It is **okay** not to have an assignment submitted each and every single day of class. This will help to free up a little time for you to catch up on grading student work, monitor student progress in your course, reach out to students/parents by phone to check in and update them on progress, respond to incoming emails, and more.

If you're utilizing a blended or flipped classroom model, this would be a good opportunity to assign asynchronous assignments, such as videos to view, self-graded assignments, assigned reading, and collaborative projects on days when students will be at home. Use your face-to-face (F2F) time in class to review information, clarify questions that students may have, engage in meaningful classroom discussions, and build on the learning that has taken place prior to stepping foot into the classroom.

If you're concerned about taking daily attendance for state-funding purposes or for your peace of mind, think about having students answer a "check-in" type of question or two on a Google Doc, Office 365 form, or another system of your choice, to turn in to you for daily attendance points.

Welcoming Your Students to Class

Now that your course announcement page is up and ready to go and the initial planning of lessons is underway, it is time to get ready to officially welcome your students into your class.

Welcome Email

A welcome email is sent out to new students as they start your course. This letter is sent to all students, even those you know have attended classes online in the past. It offers you an opportunity to introduce yourself to students and provide students and parents with course-specific information.

Your welcome email should be friendly, informative, and light on text. Think about how you respond after receiving an email that contains page after page of needless information. Do you find yourself filing it away for "later," never to read it again? I do.

Often, welcome emails include a link to your appointment scheduler, if you choose to use one, so that students can set up an appointment to connect with you prior to starting course work.

Your welcome email SHOULD include:

- Information regarding which class the email is addressing
- A friendly greeting and positive overall tone, which makes your passion for your subject area apparent and gets them excited about the course
- Directions on what to do next to "officially" get started in your class, including links to helpful videos if available
- Your contact information so they can reach out with questions or concerns
- A little about you

Your welcome email should NOT include:

- Fourteen pages of information
- Three pages of questions for them to respond to prior to getting started in class
- Threatening statements such as "You must do X or else you will lose your spot!"

- Links that are outdated or no longer work. Double-check all hyperlinks prior to sending out your welcome email.

Example Welcome Email

> Hello, Tommy,
>
> My name is Mrs. Awesome Teacher and I'll be your online Earth Space Science instructor for the 2020-2021 school year. I am so excited that you will be in my class and can't wait to connect with you and your parents/guardian soon!
>
> This year, we'll take an adventure around the globe and into outer space! We'll be learning about climate, waves, phases of the moon, the solar system, and much more!
>
> Before you jump in and start working in your class, I would love to connect with you and your parents/guardian for a few minutes. Our time together will allow me to learn a little about YOU! Then we'll discuss a few class expectations and clear up any questions you may have.
>
> At some point this week, when it's convenient for you, please reach out to me by phone or use the link below to schedule an appointment for us to connect. [**Insert appointment link here**]
>
> Looking forward to connecting with you soon!
> Mrs. Awesome Teacher
> 555-555-5555

Office Hours

Office hours are specific days and times when you are available. During this time, students can either call or log into an online classroom to ask questions, clarify information, or just say hello. No appointment necessary! Once they receive your guidance, they hang up or log out and are on their way.

Mrs. Awesome Teacher's Weekly Office Hours
I hope to see you there!
Monday 1–3 p.m.
Tuesday 9–11 a.m.
Wednesday 3–5 p.m.
Thursday 10 a.m.–12 p.m.
Friday 2–4 p.m.

It's helpful to have consistent office hours each week. This way, your students will know what to expect and can plan their school week in advance. Providing a variety of times will offer flexibility for those students who have other obligations, such as work and sports, throughout the week. It's not necessary to offer daily office hours; however, having a variety of days and times is helpful.

When initially offering your office hours to students, it may take some time for them to learn that you are there for them and to feel comfortable taking advantage of your help. It's nothing personal. If you build it, they will come.

Appointments

Sometimes, students won't feel comfortable reaching out to you by phone on a whim. It might be their first time taking an online course, and they may not be accustomed to communicating with their teacher in that way. They might be shy, or they don't want you aware of something going on at home. Sometimes, a student's day-to-day schedule is packed with school, work, sports, etc., making an impromptu call impossible.

No matter what, it's important we meet students where they are and try our best to accommodate them as much as possible. One way to work around these issues is to offer appointment hours using an online scheduling tool. Giving students the ability to schedule time with you, when it is most convenient for them and/or their parents, will help reduce the need to track them down.

There are many free tools out there that can be used within your virtual classroom, such as Office365, Google Calendar, Calendly or vCita. Check with your administration to ensure there isn't a district rule against using an outside vendor within your virtual classroom.

Possible Appointment Types

As you can imagine, much of your time is spent on calls with students and parents. What kind of calls, you ask? Well, here are some examples:

Welcome Call

As students start off in your course, it is helpful to have a one-on-one conversation with each of them to answer questions and clarify any misconceptions they may have. I'll cover welcome calls in more detail in the BRB section.

Monthly Check-In

This type of call is used to discuss the progress of a specific student in your course and should be completed with your student's parent/guardian.

One-On-One Academic Assistance

It's helpful to have an appointment that allows for students who may be struggling with course content to schedule an appointment with you for one-on-one assistance.

Exam Review Sessions

There will be times when students may not do as well as they wanted on their final exam. Giving students the opportunity to schedule an exam review session will allow for some much-needed remediation prior to them attempting the test for a second time (if your district allows retakes).

Appointment Quick Tips

- **Scatter your open appointment availability.** There's no quicker way to throw yourself off the cliff than leaving your full eight-hour workday open for appointment scheduling. Consider this your warning. If you open your appointments up for a full day, they will fill up, and that will leave you with little to no time to grade student work, respond to emails, shower, eat dinner, or remind yourself what your family looks like. Instead, you will be tethered to your computer asking yourself questions like, "What have I done?" "Will this ever end?" "Is it Friday yet?" Instead of resigning yourself to this fate, scatter your hours of availability throughout the week to ensure you have chunks of time to spend doing all the other housekeeping tasks you have as an online teacher.

- **Open your appointment blocks at times when your students seem to be most active.** Use the time stamps on assignments, student login records, or other metrics in your learning management system to discover when your students tend to engage in your online coursework.

- **Consider offering evening appointment hours one or two nights a week.** This will give those students who have obligations during daytime hours the ability to make an appointment with you. Remember, this way of learning has more flexibility than a brick-and-mortar setting, and we can adjust our days to meet students where they are.

- **Don't make appointments the only way students are allowed to contact you.** There will be times where students are stuck on an assignment or have a quick question. If you require them to make an appointment each time they need to connect with you, you will stifle learning because the lag time will often lead to student frustration and them shutting down. We want to motivate our students to keep moving in our class, not put roadblocks in front of them along their way.

- **Think about how long your appointments should be scheduled for within your app.** For example, monthly contact calls will often take less time than a phone call that has been set for one-on-one academic assistance.

- **If a student misses their scheduled call ... call THEM.** This is a learning opportunity for them and a chance for you to teach them about commitment, follow-through, and online etiquette. We teach much more than just subject matter; we teach life lessons.

- **Give students a link.** If your appointment setter provides you with a direct link to your account, post that link where students can find it quickly, such as on the front page of your virtual classroom, within text messages, and in a signature line of emails.

*****

> "The one tool or strategy that I wish I would have known from day one of online teaching is: Don't offer your appointments before noon because the middle schoolers are not yet awake!"
>
> — anonymous teacher

Remembering the Phone Shy

I think we all have at least one friend or loved one who just hates the phone. Studies show dislike of phone calls prevalent among millennials, and it's likely that Gen Z is the same.[7] So it's important to recognize that some students will feel more

---

[7] https://www.bankmycell.com/blog/why-millennials-ignore-calls

comfortable asking questions via text message or email. If they are asking questions that would be easier explained over the phone or in a F2F setting, consider creating a short video in which you share your screen and explain the concept.

Secrets of Success

- Work to ensure that students feel a sense of belonging from the first moment they log into your online course.

- Use your announcement page to share information and give students a sense of who you are as a person.

- Consider sending new students a welcome email to welcome them into their new course.

- Use an online appointment scheduler to provide students options when they want to make contact.

- Refrain from opening your appointment times up for an entire workday. Instead, designate small chunks of time throughout each day.

- Remember the phone shy and try not to take their lack of phone calls personally.

Taking Action

To give my students a sense of belonging as they start off in their online course, I will put the following processes in place:

_____

_____

_____

_____

Two items or tidbits of information I will be sure to include on my course homepage/announcement page are:

_____

_____

_____

_____

Three things I will touch base on when reaching out to students and families to welcome them into my class will be:

_____

_____

_____

_____

Providing students with the ability to set individual appointments with me is important because:

_____

_____

_____

_____

BRB: Building Relationships, BABY!

It's all about communication.

I can't tell you the number of times I have heard someone say there is no way to build strong relationships with students online like you do in a F2F, brick-and-mortar setting. And you know what? I would have said the very same thing fifteen years ago when I was teaching in a brick-and-mortar school. I pooh-poohed the idea of teaching and learning online. I thought it was a fad and would never take off. I mean, how could you possibly get to know your students online? How could you connect with them without seeing them face-to-face? I was certain that the distance would just be too much and meaningful connections would be lost along the way.

It wasn't until I started teaching ninth grade Earth Space Science online with Florida Virtual School that my entire way of thinking shifted. At first, I was skeptical, but the truth is, I pushed my skepticism aside because teaching online gave me the opportunity to stay home with my newborn.

As time went on, however, I started to see virtual learning for what it was: a way to connect one-on-one with students without the interruptions of others distracting learning. I found online teaching as a way to get to know my students on a more personal level because of their willingness to share stories and information over the phone—stories and information they never would have shared in a classroom, surrounded by their peers.

These strong bonds allowed me to keep close tabs on how my students were doing not only in my class but also outside of school. It also offered me a way to support and interact with parents on a regular basis about a variety of topics instead of just when their kiddo was driving me nuts in the classroom.

Further, it gave me the opportunity to challenge students based on where they were academically, rather than forcing them from one thing to the next just because the district's curriculum map told me to push forward. But more than anything else, teaching online gave me the ability to develop long-lasting, meaningful relationships with my online students. It's no secret to online teachers that strong relationships are the catalyst for student success!

Revisiting the Course Announcement Page

Earlier, we reviewed how to set up your course announcement page to create a social presence and start developing rapport with students. Once you've started the term, however, the page will evolve into a community space for your students. It should be a lively place with frequent updates that give your students the sense of being a part of something bigger than themselves.

Course Announcement Page Best Practices

- **Update regularly**: Your course announcement page is most effective when the information is updated on a weekly basis. If you leave the same information posted week after week, students will become disengaged and will skip past the information faster than an ad on YouTube.

- **STAR students**: Just about everyone likes to be recognized for hard work and determination! Your announcement page is the perfect place to highlight those students who are showing perseverance and growth and those who are almost done with the class. Consider choosing different aspects to highlight, such as most improved, crushing goals, and resubmission rock star rather than always highlighting the highest grade. If you choose to recognize students in your course, please be careful about publishing their full names or other identifying information. Use a first name and last initial to be mindful of students' privacy. For more information about protecting the privacy rights of students and families, see the Family Educational Rights and Privacy Act (FERPA).

Example:
★ ★ Star Students! ★ ★
Amy K., Tina W., Michael M., Andrew M.

- **Let your creative juices flow**: Make this space your own, make your presence known, and don't be afraid to try new things from week to week. Bust out those cute virtual borders and die-cut letters! Facebook offers a variety of fun groups to join to get creative ideas from educators around the world.

- **Be mindful of graphics or humor that may offend**: Something you find funny may make students feel uncomfortable or demeaned, so be sensitive when selecting graphics and humor to share. What might be funny or well taken in a face-to-face classroom setting may not go over as well in a virtual classroom.

- **Stay flexible**: Because our online world offers flexibility that a traditional classroom doesn't, we want to avoid phrases that suggest limited availability, such as "NO CALLS," "NOT AVAILABLE," or "DO NOT CALL."

- **Maintain privacy**: Keep any confidential information about students, including grades, contact information, or teacher notes, within your district websites. Keeping a handwritten log or personal website about students' personal information would be frowned upon.

Welcome Calls: The Golden Egg

In the last chapter, we discussed using a welcome email to introduce yourself to your new online learners. Part of that email included asking students and parents to reach out to you for an initial phone call. This phone call, when it happens, is one of the most important opportunities to engage with your students.

However, to get the most out of this call, you **must** spend the majority of your time allowing your students to share information about themselves. Unwritten rule #1549 of online teaching states:

One shall not dominate conversations with students.

Most young adults love the opportunity to share information about themselves, so this should not be an issue. Ask them questions, such as:

- Why are you taking this online course?
- Have you ever taken an online course before?
- What is something you are excited about when it comes to taking a class online?
- Do you have any siblings?
- What pets do you have?
- Who do you live with?
- What are some of your favorite hobbies?

As you're asking these questions, or others that better fit your students' age group, jot down their answers for future use. You can use a simple Excel file or other note-taking tool. Remember, use first names and last initials to follow FERPA guidelines. Save this information for the next time you connect. This will allow you to circle back and ask questions specifically relating to what they previously shared with you. "How is your brother Sam doing?" "Did you get any more kittens?" "How is soccer practice going?"

By taking a few moments to document some simple personal information about each of your students, you will set yourself up for success when it comes to building stronger relationships with your online learners. You will be shocked at how much they remember about you too. Don't be afraid to share about your own likes, dislikes, hobbies, and family members. By doing so, you will become more human to them and less of a robot on the other side of the computer screen.

> There's a thin line between asking some harmless questions and coming across as an FBI interrogator. Keep the number of questions to under ten and keep the tone conversational. Remember, you want to learn about them, not gather intel.

Your initial phone call should last no more than fifteen to twenty minutes. The fact is, about 90 percent of the information you share during this time about your class will most likely be forgotten. Students often go into information overload and start to respond with yes/no answers. When this happens, it's time to cut your conversation short.

Remember, you will be communicating with your students on a regular basis and there will be other opportunities to remind them of your classroom expectations. A follow-up email, which includes the highlights of your conversation, can be helpful!

Connecting through Phone Calls

Throughout your relationship with students, you will have many phone calls after the welcome call. One of the first things I learned when I started teaching online was how important the first ten seconds of each and every phone call with your students are.

I will never forget calling a student who hadn't worked for a while. The moment she answered, I started rambling on about how she hadn't been working and if she didn't submit work soon, I would have to withdraw her from the course. Before I could take a deep breath to get on to my next soapbox, the student informed me that one of her parents had passed away two weeks before from cancer, and that's why she hadn't submitted work.

That was a moment I will never forget, one that has made me a better online teacher.

The first ten seconds of every phone call you make should start with "How are you doing?" or "Is everything going okay?" You might be the ONLY person in their day who asks them how they are. When we show that we care, it is the most important way to build strong relationships with our kiddos. Those strong bonds won't form if we are only focused on their lack of work or poor motivation.

There have been times when I've called a student to discuss one thing but ended up just talking to the student about a challenge they were experiencing at home or with a good friend. My call about their lack of work can take place another time. At that moment when they are upset, they aren't going to absorb anything I share about their progress in the online course.

And to be honest, the most important thing at that moment is helping them through a challenging time when they might not have anyone else to turn to.

Playing Cat and Mouse

Phone tag, or the game of cat and mouse, happens frequently when teaching online. It might be due to a student's lack of access to a working phone, scheduling conflicts, apprehension over using the phone, or the fear of getting in trouble. Here are a few best practices when reaching out to students who are not responding to your attempts to make contact:

- Reach out at different times of the day. If the student is in a traditional school building during daytime hours, you'll be spinning your wheels by calling earlier in the day. Try calling in the evening instead.

- When leaving a voicemail, refrain from stating that you are calling about lack of work or a poor grade. NOBODY will want to call you back when that's coming their way.

- Send the student a quick text to let them know that you'd like to check in. Including a fun GIF or Bitmoji will lighten the tone of the text and make it friendlier.

- Try the CHA-CHA method. Call, Harass, Annoy until a student calls you out of spite! This should be saved as a last resort and for only the most extreme cases.

Bonding with Students through Email

Relationship building isn't restricted to just phone conversations. Making sure your emails are inviting and that they encourage students to reach out to you with questions is another way to keep the lines of communication open and continue developing a relationship. Asking students questions about themselves and the things they enjoy doing in life, as part of your email, gives students a way to share with you and will help strengthen your online relationships.

Be mindful of blanket emails that are sent out to your entire class. Regularly sending form letters or mail-merge communication where information is autopopulated can take away from the meaningfulness of your communication. Instead of students looking to your emails and feeling as though they are meant only for them, they will tag them as spam and not pay close attention to what you have to say because *everyone* is receiving the same message.

To build strong relationships with online learners, we have to strive to make each student feel like the only student we have in class. Pushing the same blanket statements out to the masses, time and time again, does not paint that picture.

True or False?

I have sent three emails to all the students who haven't submitted work in the last two weeks. I have done my part.

FALSE

Sending an email is a passive communication technique. If you're doing the same thing over and over with the same result, stop it! That is the definition of insanity. In a situation where a student is not working in your class or hasn't been communicating with you online, an initial email is great, but a follow-up phone call is even better.

One way to manage the task of calling students missing in action is to count up the number of students who have not submitted work in the last two weeks and divide that number by five, the number of days in the week. That will break up the number of outgoing phone calls into smaller, more digestible parts. A best practice would be to reach out to any nonworking students within the first seven to ten days of submitting no work.

Supporting ELL students

It can be a challenge to support and establish relationships with students who are English Language Learners. In a classroom setting, perhaps you had supports in place where ELL students had a resource person in the room with them to help with translating information. It is unlikely you will have the same level of support available to you on a daily basis in an online environment. Interacting online with students who have difficulty understanding what you are trying to teach can lead to frustrations for both the student and teacher. Discussions over the phone or written directions provided throughout your course can be challenging. For a more in-depth study on connecting with ELL students, I highly recommend Mawi Asgedom's book, *Empowering English Learners For Classroom Success: 6 Keys to Academic and Social-Emotional Growth*.

In the meantime, here are a few tips I learned over the years that helped to meet the needs of these students while ensuring equally strong bonds are formed with them too:

- If you have someone on staff who is fluent in the language, consider asking that teammate to help with translations.

- Use Google Translate or other tools such as TalkingPoints when writing and/or responding to emails and text messages.

- Open Google Translate in your web browser or on your cell phone so that you can translate within seconds in a text.

- When possible, provide students several options for showing mastery of coursework so that if they're uncomfortable with one option, they have others from which to choose. This is a good practice for all students.

True or False?

If a student doesn't return my calls, they just don't care.

FALSE

There are a variety of reasons why a student, parent, or guardian doesn't return a phone call. Work schedules, stressors at home, fear of what they might hear, ignoring calls from numbers they don't recognize, attempts to get work in before talking with you—the list is endless.

If a student or parent/guardian isn't responding to your phone calls, send the parent/guardian a text that only says the following:

*Hello, is this the parent or guardian of **[insert student name here]**?*

Say NOTHING else. It's virtually impossible for a parent/guardian to hold off on responding to a text like that. Sneaky, right? I know!

Bottom line: Try different strategies and don't get stuck on one way of doing something. Send emails, make calls, use text messaging. If one thing isn't working, try something else! But, no matter what, don't give up on your students.

Building Classroom Community

At the start of the last chapter, we touched on social presence. Another way to help build social presence is through establishing your classroom community.

It can be challenging to find opportunities to engage and interact with your virtual learners. If you worked in a brick-and-mortar setting in the past, you may feel distant from your students or like you're missing that special connection you felt within the four walls of your classroom. The good news is, there are many ways in which you can engage with your students online and build strong bonds. You just have to be intentional and use your super creative teacher juices!

For me, being creative meant pushing the limits and doing things that would catch my students off guard or intrigue them enough to take part. On and off throughout the year, it was common practice for me to present challenges to my students to help motivate them to finish up their current semester of work.

One year, right before winter break, I told my students that if fifty of them finished up before we shut down for the holiday, I would dress up in footie pajamas and head to the local mall to read a story to random children, alongside Santa

Claus. To sweeten the deal, I promised to document the entire experience in pictures and video to share with them.

My students rallied and accomplished the goal, which is how I found myself sitting next to Santa reading *The Night Before Christmas*, with pigtails, big, red, painted-on lips, and long-johns-style footie pajamas ... in Florida. My students loved it and were excited to see what was up my sleeve next.

The author reading to children with Santa

The following year, I challenged my students to take part in a week-long team effort. I promised that if the entire class submitted 100 assignments for grading between Monday and Friday of that week, I would shove 100 mini marshmallows in my mouth at one time. The plan worked as I'd hoped, and they all submitted the assignments. Of course, there was a downside, something I quickly learned as I drooled, snorted, gagged, and laughed my way to a mouthful of 100 mini marshmallows. It was totally worth it. It was something I, and I hope the students, will never forget.

The author eating 100 mini marshmallows

You don't have to dress up and read stories with Santa during a Florida winter's day or pack your mouth full of marshmallows to get the attention of your students. The point is, be fearless and try new things to connect with your online learners. Give them opportunities to see that you're more than just a voice on the other end of the line—you are a real person!

Take a moment to think about all the different ways you interact and build a sense of community with your students while in the traditional classroom: high fives as students walk in the front door, circle time, small reading groups, group discussions, and so on. Now, think about how those different interactions translate into the virtual world. Want some ideas? Here you go:

Use your virtual classroom to build a sense of belonging

- Community bulletin boards using apps such as Padlet
- Individual videos to share with the class
- Highlighting STAR STUDENTS of the week
- Create a weekly video letting students know what to expect for the week, sharing what you did over the weekend, or asking them to respond to a question about themselves.

- Collaborative online projects using Office 365 PowerPoint slides
- Post pictures of yourself doing the things you love the most in life, such as skydiving, traveling, reading, surfing, and dancing.
- With student approval, share pictures of student artwork, hobbies, and pets. As always, be cautious of posting student names.

Keep the conversation going

- Play a game of trivia through Zoom.
- Offer class office hours to allow students to log in and visit with others.
- Incorporate discussion posts, polls, collaborative online activities, and feedback to engage your students in conversation.
- Choose a current event and ask your students to come join you online to discuss the topic.
- Call students to say hello! They'll love connecting with you without other distractions.
- Use feedback to encourage conversation by asking reflective questions.
- Encourage students to join you during your office hours to review incorrect work and/or to ask questions.

Building Teacher/Parent Relationships

Nothing makes your job easier than when a parent/guardian is in your corner. They are important allies to have and building rapport with them is not as hard as you think.

Bragging about your online cherubs to their parents/guardians is a surefire way to establish strong teacher/parent connections. Parents often only hear from teachers when things aren't going well, such as when a student misbehaves, cheats, or fails to submit work. It is essential to reach out when things are going well, not just when there is an issue. Take the time to acknowledge growth or success, no matter how small it may be, to build trust and develop a partnership between you, your students, and your students' parents.

I once had this student William. He was a senior who lacked motivation to do anything in school. He checked out and was ready for his high school career to be over. What William didn't fully understand was that his high school career was bound to last a lot longer if he didn't get his butt in gear. One week, after many attempted phone calls, text messages, and emails regarding his lackluster work ethic, he submitted two assignments. I immediately picked up the phone and called home. Mom answered, knew it was me, and quickly stated, "I know, he hasn't done anything. I'm still trying to get him to work on my end."

You see, Mom and I had built a strong relationship throughout the semester and she was now on my team. It was at that moment that I got to deliver the news that in fact, William had submitted work and it was clear that he put forth a lot of effort on the work that he turned in. I asked for Mom to put my call on speaker with William in the room. And then I bragged and bragged about how well he had done on his work and how proud and excited I was to see such effort.

The next day, I received two more stellar assignments, and William worked to complete not only my course but another online course he was taking at the same time. He turned it around and was able to graduate on time with the rest of his senior class.

It was about three weeks later that I received an email from William thanking me for having faith in him and never giving up on him as my student. He also shared that my phone call home to him and his mom meant so much, as the only phone calls he'd gotten up to that point were ones telling him all of his inadequacies as a student.

> Online educators have found that parents tend to be more responsive to text messages than any other type of contact. However, it is important to make that one-on-one contact from time to time and not always rely on written communication. There is no substitution for seeing a parent's or student's face or hearing their voice.

Staying Connected with Coworkers

It was a tradition in one of the schools I worked in that on Fridays, after all the students filed out to head home, the teachers would come out into the hallway and debrief about their week. It was always such a great feeling to know you weren't alone and others were feeling the same frustrations as you in the classroom.

It was also a time for us to share the *great* things that were happening with our students that others may not always have the opportunity to see. You may have experienced the same type of "water-cooler talk" at the copy machine, mailbox area, or staff lounge. These moments are essential to building relationships and allow opportunities to share best practices and learn from our fellow educators.

When working remotely, these water-cooler moments can still take place; you just have to be more intentional and creative to ensure that they happen! You can try to:

- Hold a weekly online meeting with your fellow teachers to just hang out.

- Create a text group containing your work besties to keep in constant contact.

- Send an email to someone you haven't connected with in a bit, just to say hello.

- Give someone a call! In my experience, folks will often say they are doing great or won't have any questions when prompted via email. However, when given a call they're more likely to be candid with how they're feeling and share more openly and honestly.

- Use tools and apps such as Skype, Slack or Yammer in Office 365 to create a way for teachers to reach out to each other quickly.

Don't become an island. If you feel isolated or distant from others and need to reconnect, picking up the phone to say hello is a great way to make that happen. And no matter what outlet you choose, remember to observe student privacy protection and be careful that it doesn't become a negative complaint session each time you reach out. We need to be a positive force and support for one another. Engaging in constant complaining can bring others down.

Curbing Your Negativity

Our days are difficult enough without negative attitudes shining a horrible light on anything that might be remotely difficult or controversial. While critical thinking and courage are important to an online teaching career, doing so in a positive way is essential. It's vital that you keep a positive attitude and steer away from sucking the life out of others, just to complain or make yourself feel better. Likewise, it's vital you don't allow anyone else's negativity to drag you down.

When I think about teachers who are positive, one particular colleague comes to mind. I can always count on her to be a positive force to those around her. Her positive attitude and upbeat nature are infectious, and we all need more of that!

If you find yourself cornered by a Negative Nelly, try to control the situation by:

- Turning the conversation around to focus on the positives and benefits of a situation or next steps in resolving it.

- Letting them know they have five minutes to vent and then you want to discuss ways to make things better.

- Simply limiting your exposure to this person as much as possible.

Don't allow Nelly's issues to become your own! Remember how you feel about the topic and try not to allow the heated comments of others to sway you.

Secrets of Success

- Building strong relationships with students and their parents is the most important thing we can do as online educators.

- Allow students the opportunity to share stories and information about themselves, when possible, to strengthen bonds and get a sense of how they are doing on a regular basis.

- Parents and guardians are an ally, and with their support, you can work as a team to support their child and guide them to success.

- Find creative ways to connect with your coworkers on a regular basis for those water-cooler moments.

- Provide students options when it comes to showing content mastery.

- Keep connected, even when you feel like your efforts are in vain.

- Avoid Negative Nellies and don't let yourself become one.

Taking Action

To keep the lines of communication open with my students and parents, I will use these three strategies:

_____

_____

_____

_____

To keep connected with my coworkers while working remotely, I plan to:

_____

_____

_____

_____

Something specific I can do to help build strong relationships with my online students is:

_____

_____

_____

_____

How can building strong relationships with my students' parents help to ensure the success of the students in my online class?

_____

_____

_____

_____

If a Negative Nelly virtually corners me, I will try to take control of the situation by:

_____

_____

_____

_____

CSI: Customer Service Integration

All in a day's work.

Often, as we leave part-time high school gigs in retail behind, we assume that we are done with all that customer-service stuff we had to do before we went into teaching. But that's not the case.

As a teacher, especially one in a virtual environment, you provide customer service all day, every day, to your students, their parents, your administration, and your colleagues. So, all those skills you thought you could leave behind? Time to dust them off and see how much they help in your new career.

Watch Your Tone: Email Etiquette

Tone is important both in emails and text messages. Paying attention to how the other person may perceive your message is a big part of customer service. Some of the best online teachers I know refer to their email etiquette as the "Mary Poppins technique." Using this technique, they avoid:

- WRITING IN ALL CAPS. This comes across as screaming in an email or text message.

- Using threatening phrases. This may include phrases like, "You must do this or else ..." or "If you don't do this, you will be dropped from this class." Stay away from threats in emails. These types of conversations are better had on the phone or on video than in an email where the tone can be read much differently than intended.

- Delaying their response for more than twenty-four hours. Often a long delay in responding can cause the other person anxiety and intensify an already stressful situation.

- Trying to prove or stand up for yourself through email. In these sensitive situations, it's often best to connect online or on the phone, using some tips from the CSI section.

More Words and Terms to Avoid

Sometimes, the words that we choose can be taken in ways we don't intend. To keep an appropriate, customer-service-oriented tone in emails to parents, students, and colleagues, avoid the following:

FINE
"Is it okay if I take two more days to finish the report?"
"Fine."

Even if you mean, "That's fine / go ahead / no problem," *fine* has negative connotations. With the same number of letters, you can type "okay" or "sure."

NO
"Is our meeting in Zoom at 1 p.m.?"
"No, it's at 3."

If someone writes to you and asks a question and includes the wrong information, you can simply respond using the correct information. There's no need for the "no."

PER MY LAST
"How do I document this type of phone call?"
"Per my last email, you would want to do X, Y, and Z."

I know it's annoying to have to repeat yourself, but things get busy in our virtual world. Give others some grace and provide a direct answer to their questions rather than pointing out that you've already told them something.

Learn to Walk Away

A few months ago, I went shopping at a big-box retailer. After spending way more money than I'd planned, I headed home with my goodies. But there were only two items I really cared about: my bagels and salmon. These were things I rarely bought for myself, and I was so excited and couldn't wait to get home, make a cream cheese and lox bagel, and shove it directly into my face.

As I unloaded my trunk, I soon realized that the lox never made it into my car! It was disappointing to say the least. The next day I returned to the store with my receipt, to share with them that my item was left behind. The customer-service rep I shared my story with looked directly into my eyes and said, "It wasn't our fault that the fish never made it into your car."

During times like these, it's better to keep those types of thoughts and feelings tucked right inside your brain, never to pass through the soft skin of your lips. In fact, there are lots of times like that. Have you ever had a moment where you are in a heated discussion and before you can control yourself, something comes out of your mouth that you regret two seconds later? Yes, me too! You might have wished that your mouth came with a backspace or delete key. Especially in our virtual work, we have to make sure we don't pull our verbal triggers too fast, which can easily happen via email.

Imagine rolling out of bed, sliding on your fuzzy slippers, grabbing your *#1 Teacher* coffee mug filled with your favorite brew, and snuggling in to dig through those late-night emails that came in after you shut things down at 11 p.m. The first email that snags your attention is one with the subject line, "Important: Open Immediately." At this point, you should know that nothing good will come of this, but still you open the email and begin reading.

As you skim through five paragraphs of bold and underlined text, your blood starts to boil. You read the email in a high-pitched voice in your head with the right side of your upper lip curled up like a snarling dog. By the end of the email, you've already started to conjure up your response to the sender, which contains two level tablespoons of sass and one heaping cup of whoop-a—STOP. Do not go any further. Abort the mission and step aside. Slowly back away from the computer and take your coffee mug with you.

It's never a good time to respond to an email when you're upset, frustrated, ready to claw someone's eyes out, *and* low on caffeine. Trust me, it will not end well.

Unwritten rule #345 of online teaching states:

One shall not respond to emails, phone calls, or text messages when enraged.

My suggestion is to close the email, text, or voicemail, and give yourself one full day to focus on something else and remove yourself from the situation. After you've calmed down, circle back to the message when you're in a better state of mind. It can also be helpful to have someone read over your email/text response prior to sending it or to role-play the phone call conversation so that you have some practice and won't feel so caught off guard.

No matter what, collect yourself, assume the best of intentions, and respond after you have had time to simmer down.

These types of sticky situations don't just happen via email; however, it is much easier to take a step back and cool off when they do. Sometimes, these conversations happen over the phone. These are the challenges that will really test your skills. These are the challenges that will remind you of why you are grateful you teach online.

So, what do you do when you have an irate parent on the other end of the line? You listen. That's right. You give the parent the chance to get it all out.

When the parent is done, your goal is not to prove your point but to move things forward. This is not the time to defend the classroom expectations you have put into place or play devil's advocate. Most often, a parent's frustration has

NOTHING to do with you. And, the reality is, many times the other person won't care how you feel about what was shared. The other person really just needed to get it out.

The most important thing that we can do is work to move things forward. To help deescalate upset parents and make forward progress, I use statements such as:

> "I hear you and understand why you would feel frustrated. What can we do **moving forward** to make this better?"
>
> "It's clear that you are upset. How can we **work together** to ensure your child is **successful** in my course?"
>
> "I am sorry you are feeling that way. However, I am sure that with the two of us **working together** on this, we'll be able to support your child and **help them reach their goals**."

On a side note, if a phone conversation or email interaction is abusive in nature, you should not engage. Forward the email to your admin team or higher-ups so they can handle it administratively. If on the phone, tell the person you are hanging up and they are more than welcome to call your principal or direct supervisor. It is not OK for you to be verbally abused or treated in an unprofessional manner. Please do not tolerate this. I can guarantee that is not in your job description.

Assume Others Have the Best Intentions

A wise woman once said to me, "Try to always assume that others have the best intentions." This has stuck with me, and it's something I try to remind myself of, especially when working through difficult situations.

Assume others have the best intentions. When you receive an email that seems short or insensitive, take a step back and shift your mindset. Sometimes just the way we read something can give it an edge that the sender never intended. If you look at it through the lens of the other person, assuming the best intent and coming from a good place, it can be easier to take in the real meaning of what that individual is trying to say.

Secrets of Success

- Never respond to an email while angry or feeling frustrated.

- Always double-check to be sure your salmon makes it into your car at the grocery store.

- When working through difficult conversations with parents, always keep the focus on how you can move things forward.

- Pay attention to the tone of your communication.

- Assume the best intentions, even during the most difficult situations.

- Before hitting send on a difficult email, have a colleague look it over to check the tone.

- Stay away from statements such as "per my last email."

Taking Action

When communicating with a parent who is obviously upset, I will use the following customer-service strategies:

_____

_____

_____

_____

If a student or parent becomes irate and abusive during a phone call or via email, I will do the following:

_____

_____

_____

_____

One way I can provide stellar customer service to my students and their parents is by:

_____

_____

_____

_____

LMAO: Leading Meetings All Online

"I really have to get out of these PJs and show my sweaty face on screen for live lessons, professional learning communities, and staff meetings?"

Another aspect of teaching online is that a lot of the work you're accustomed to handling in a face-to-face (F2F) setting will now be online. Professional learning communities (PLCs), staff meetings, IEP meetings, team meetings, presenting lessons, and more will now be online, often with a web camera aimed at your face.

Even if you're camera shy, it's absolutely critical that you put yourself on camera regularly to help with engagement. If you're not used to being on camera, practice with friends and family. Push your professional growth by getting used to this new medium and be a model showing students that it's good to try new things, even if it makes you uncomfortable. It can be scary and make you feel uneasy, but that means you are growing. It's pushing you outside of your comfort zone.

And after you've grown used to online meetings and cameras, you may find you enjoy online meetings far more than F2F meetings—especially if you follow these tips.

Quick Online Meeting Tips

The first rule of thumb in creating a happy workday is not to schedule back-to-back meetings. Doing so can be exhausting and overwhelming. Worse, if one meeting runs over, it will throw off the next meeting, and then the next. It's a good idea to give yourself a little buffer in between each one—and enough time to send a follow-up email, stretch your legs, use the restroom, or grab another cup of coffee or a quick bite to eat.

Know how to dress right because getting dressed isn't entirely optional in the virtual setting. If you're going to be sitting without getting up during your meeting, you can get away with wearing a nice shirt and those comfy, ratty pajama bottoms you've had since college.

My husband works outside the house and is gone from early in the morning until six every evening. I'm in bed when he leaves and often lying on the couch unwinding when he returns. So how is it that he always knows when I've had a meeting? Could it be that my hair is brushed and I have makeup on? Actually, it's often due to the nice shirt I'm wearing paired with my poop emoji PJ bottoms and fuzzy animal socks. Have a good selection of nice shirts available, and you won't even have to do laundry that often.

After getting dressed (i.e., putting on a clean shirt), you need to look behind you. No, this isn't a horror movie, but it could be if you surprise students and colleagues with an unexpected reflection of your backside. Take a look at the perimeter of your camera shot to make sure everything in view is work appropriate. Consider book titles on shelves, magazines on tables, and reflective surfaces to be sure the coast is clear.

Or, you can cut down on interference by having your back to the wall whenever you're on camera. You can also use your wall as a bulletin board to hang anchor charts, class announcements, and other useful materials.

Once you've checked out your rear view, it's time to think about your front view, and that means watching your camera angles. Trust me, nobody wants to see up your nose during an online meeting or lesson. To ensure no one does, place your monitor at eye level or slightly above. This way, you give yourself a fighting chance of keeping your bat cave private. It also tends to be a more flattering angle in general, which is a nice bonus!

Being late is never good. While online meetings may not have a commute, they can have other issues. So, make sure you always log in early. No matter how many online meetings you've attended and how often you've used the software, you will, at some point, have technical issues—probably when you're least prepared for it. To help prevent these imminent issues from delaying your meetings, log in fifteen to twenty minutes early, every time.

No one wants to do a Zoom meeting with a bunch of zombies, so be sure to engage in the meetings you attend. This could mean responding in the chat box that is often provided or asking/responding to a question. Try to keep your comments and questions focused on what is being shared in the meeting and not on your own agenda. You will find out why this intentional interaction is so important when you are on the other side and hosting a meeting yourself.

For those who need to reduce background noise, headphones are a great option. In fact, you could be wearing your headphones for a long time each day, so think about what's most comfortable for you—headphones that cover your entire ear, or earbuds? Also consider the convenience of Bluetooth connections over cords.

Oh, and if you have teenage children, hide the headphones away at the end of your workday. I've gone through four pairs of earbuds this school year already and, at the time of this writing, we still have a few months to go!

Challenges of Online Meetings

F2F meetings have their benefits, but they also have their fair share of challenges. When you attend them, you have to figure out what to wear each time, and I mean, like, an entire outfit. The commute time to and from the school eats up a portion of your day, and it can be awkward to know where to sit without hurting someone's feelings.

In a F2F meeting, the surrounding noises can be overwhelming if you are sensitive to things like people chatting with each other or making comments under their breath. It can be difficult to hear if the speakers aren't using a microphone or aren't using their teachers' voices to reach every corner of the room. And there's always a naysayer in the bunch—if you get stuck next to that person, it can be a real energy suck.

Online meetings remove all those drawbacks. They also have added benefits, like giving you the ability to record the sessions to review at another time or save a copy of the chat box so that it can be reviewed later.

But that doesn't mean online meetings are perfect. In fact, you may find that online meetings have their own set of frustrations. When you know what these are in advance, you can counteract them.

- Technology doesn't always play nicely, so you might have difficulty logging into the online session.

- Sometimes you will be on camera for the entire time, which can be draining because you are ON.

- If you have family members at home, this will definitely be the time they walk by in the background with no clothes on.

- Dogs will bark, kids will scream, and someone will knock on your door during the meeting.

- There are moments when audio or video might not work properly.

- Conversation can lag depending on the host's ability to engage participants—and technology's ability to keep up.

- People logging in late can distract the other participants already in the room.

- Comments and questions entered in a chat box area can be difficult to manage when there are many participants in the room. Items can be overlooked or missed.

Here are some handy tips to help you smooth your online meeting experience, both as host and participant:

- Hang a sign outside of your office space letting family know when you are in a meeting. Works well with older children. A DO NOT DISTURB template can be found in the Resources area of this book.

- Little ones at home? Hide in a bathroom with the door closed when in a meeting. Just kidding (well, sort of).

- Ask family members, daycare providers, or babysitters for their availability during scheduled meetings to take that stressor off your plate and give you the ability to focus. If this is not an option, you will have to do the best you can and allow yourself some grace.

- Set up a play area near you for little ones where they are contained and occupied.

- Arrange a playdate with a friend, family member or another virtual teacher during meeting times where kids can play and you can sneak away to attend your meeting.

- Log in to your meeting fifteen to twenty minutes early in case something doesn't go as planned. This will give you some time to test your system and troubleshoot.

- If possible, mute all participants during the meeting when sharing information. That will cut down on background noise.

- Try to schedule deliveries to your home for times when you do not have a meeting scheduled.

Keep things minimal in your home office. Consider having a printer, a binder for things you want to print out and keep organized, a landline if your cell service is spotty, and high-speed internet all located in a central area. If you have the room to have an office in a space that can be closed off at night, like a guest bedroom, it makes it much easier to shut things down and walk away at the end of your "day."

It's not required, however. I have worked from my couch for fifteen years surrounded by crazy kids and a TV on 90 percent of the time to provide me with mindless background noise. What works for some may not work for others.

Finally, remember that most of your colleagues are in the same boat as you. Be understanding with them and yourself when meetings don't go entirely as planned.

Do you miss that face-to-face interaction with your coworkers? Reach out and have an online meeting with them to chat about something that isn't work related. Why not invite several fellow educators to join you for an online "happy hour" or "lunch & learn" session at the end of the workweek?

Remember, your conferencing tools are not only used to deliver information but more importantly, to help build relationships with students and colleagues alike. In a virtual setting, you have to be more intentional about building those relationships.

Prepping Student Meetings and Live Lessons

You've reached the chapter that covers specifics on hosting live lessons and collaborations! This is the best part! This is why we teach: to work with students and see those *aha* moments!

Being in a classroom with students does have its benefits. Nothing beats those morning hugs and high fives at the start of the day. In a F2F setting, it's easy to observe students' body language to get a sense of when they are struggling, have tuned out, or are shutting down. It's common to place students into small groups for collaborative projects and meaningful discussions in the classroom. The good news is, all of these things can still happen in virtual classrooms and during our online interactions with students.

As exciting as it is, the thought of live lessons and student meetings might also bring you the most anxiety. What will you do with students when they log in? How do you teach classroom-based lessons in an online format? And the biggie, how do you keep them engaged?

Here's the deal. You can teach the same content you did in a traditional classroom, but it will have a different look and feel in order to better communicate and engage in a virtual setting. It's important to be flexible and recognize that it takes time to develop to the high level of teaching you were able to provide in a brick-and-mortar classroom. But, in time, you'll learn new skills that will help you enhance your online environment. It's all about those baby steps.

Scheduling

We can be flexible as virtual educators, but there are some places where consistency is definitely important. One of those areas is in scheduling your live lessons and your weekly office hours, if you are offering those. If your dates and times for these events are always changing, it will make it more difficult for students to stay organized from one week to the next.

If you're planning on offering weekly office hours, it's helpful to be consistent with your offerings but provide students with choices.

Example:
If you schedule office hours on Monday and Wednesdays from 10 to 11 a.m., some of your students may never be available for a session at that time of day.

However, if you offer Monday and Wednesday from 10 to 11 a.m. and then another session on Thursdays from 2 to 3 p.m., you're giving another option for those students who need a later starting time.

If you're not even sure where to begin in terms of scheduling, you may want to poll your students and their families at the start of the school year to see what they would prefer. That data can be used to drive your decisions.

Be sure to alert your students in advance of any online meetings. Send your students a reminder the day before and the day of your meeting, if possible. The calendar within your LMS may also offer reminder options for scheduled events such as live lessons. There are free and low-cost texting apps available that allow you to input a group of numbers and send batch text messages to do a group reminder. One Call Now, Google Voice, and WhatsApp are just a few apps available out there.

Post your meeting times or office hours on the front page of your course too. Reach out to students individually if you notice they are not showing up to your class meetings or required sessions. If students feel like they can fly under the radar and not be called out for missing class meetings, they will often push the limits and do it over and over again.

> When students avoid meetings and sessions, you have to pay close attention to not only what is said but also to what is NOT being said.

Online Meeting and Live Lesson Tech Prep

The first thing is to find a district-approved web conferencing tool that you're comfortable using. Once your district tells you what tech you can use, you'll want to find out the max number of participants who can join a session, then learn how to do the following:

- ❏ Mute all the students at once.
- ❏ Remove the mic use from all students at once.
- ❏ Remove the video option from all students.
- ❏ Secure the students' login process.
- ❏ Remove students' ability to write on the screen.
- ❏ Take attendance at the end of your session.
- ❏ Record your meeting and share a link to a recording with others. Make sure you follow FERPA rules and that your district allows you to have student names appear in the recording.

Practice Your Tech

You wouldn't fly a plane without proper training and practice, would you? Well, you might not be bringing your students up to 30,000 feet, but it's still important to practice using your online tools before introducing them to your students. Ask coworkers to log in with you to try things out. Things to practice include:

- Logging into your meeting
- MUTING participants
- Sharing your screen
- Providing students with a microphone
- Removing the microphone from participants
- Sharing your video camera
- Recording a session (in compliance with your district and FERPA)
- Removing video options from students
- Removing a student from your session
- Using a whiteboard
- Restricting access to drawing on the whiteboard

- Removing drawing from your screen
- Last but not least, be sure to remove files and nonrelevant open tabs from your desktop prior to sharing your screen with others

Believe me when I tell you that you cannot overprepare for online lessons. You may think that practicing student removal and whiteboard use is overdoing it, but the first time a student draws something inappropriate on the whiteboard during your lesson, you'll wish you'd trained harder.

Whiteboards are not for the faint of heart. If you plan to use them in your meetings and lessons, your number one skill should be removing drawings from your screen without missing a beat. When I was just starting out, a student drew a certain part of the male anatomy on the virtual whiteboard, and I panicked, promptly ending the meeting instead of just removing the artist of questionable taste. I offered no explanation to anyone and pretended like the session never took place.

If you really want to freak yourself out while also seeing firsthand how important practice is, record your fifth online meeting and play it back in a few weeks. You might be astounded at the number of times you say, "Umm," "So," "Like," and "Okay." Listening to yourself is an opportunity to grow ... right after you lift your chin off the ground.

It will make you keenly aware of the little things you never noticed about your delivery and help you get better at presenting material in any virtual setting. And remember, all of this is totally normal and to be expected!

One Starfish at a Time

> One day a man was walking along the beach when he noticed a boy picking something up and gently throwing it into the ocean.
>
> Approaching the boy, he asked, "What are you doing?"
>
> The youth replied, "Throwing starfish back into the ocean. The surf is up, and the tide is going out. If I don't throw them back, they'll die."
>
> "Son," the man said, "don't you realize there are miles and miles of beach and hundreds of starfish? You can't make a difference!"
>
> After listening politely, the boy bent down, picked up another starfish, and threw it back into the surf. Then, smiling at the man, he said, "I made a difference for that one."
>
> — Story as related by the Ataturk Society of America, based on an essay by Loren Eiseley

Virtual classrooms don't have the same constraints as brick-and-mortar. Sometimes, you might send out 100 invitations for a live lesson or online meeting and have only ten students meander through your virtual doors. Why? Well, there could be a number of reasons.

Occasionally, the times we set for our meetings don't align with their scheduling needs at home. They could be watching siblings during the day or sharing a computer with other family members and not be able to log in to an online meeting. They may be ill, working within another course, or even attending a different live lesson. Some students might not have access to a camera or working microphone on their computers. Sometimes, situations at home interfere with them being able to log into your session, and they won't always share that information with you.

It's important to always remember that we don't know what's going on in their worlds. We may not be privy to some of their challenges at home, including things they may feel embarrassed about or want to keep private. Don't get discouraged. If you're consistent with your offerings, they WILL come. It just might take them a little while to adjust to how your online class is run and scheduled. The last thing you want to do is base the frequency of your live-lesson offerings on the number of students who attend the first few meetings.

While only one or two starfish might attend your live lessons and meetings, those who do deserve your full attention, guidance, and support. I would suggest keeping mandatory weekly synchronous meetings to a minimum while making sure that those you hold are intentional, well planned, engaging, and are used to check in on the well-being of your online learners. You can also offer the option of providing a recording of your session to those students who are unable to attend.

Another strategy for getting students to log into live-lesson sessions is to allow attendance to take the place of an assignment in the course. If the live lesson directly covers the learning goals, benchmarks, and/or standards that the student would be expected to meet when completing the online lesson, and they can show you they understand the information, consider allowing them to replace the grade with their live-lesson participation grade. To maintain consistency throughout your school, you will want to clear this with your school's leadership team.

It's extremely important not to let low attendance discourage you from flexible online meeting and lesson offerings. After all, these meetings give students an opportunity to be social with other online learners and learn life skills they may use in the future. When you consider that the number of employees working remotely at least one time per week has grown almost 400 percent since 2010, getting used to communicating, relating, and presenting themselves online can be critical skills for their future success.[8]

Secrets of Success

- Use the MUTE ALL button when hosting online meetings.

- Be careful not to schedule back-to-back online meetings.

- Practice using your online conferencing tool with friends, family, or coworkers to get the hang of the tools available to you.

- Log into online meetings in advance to ensure technology is playing nice and that you are prepared to begin on time.

- Use a DO NOT DISTURB sign on an office, closet, or bathroom door when in meetings or student calls. Look in the Resources section for one you can use now!

---

[8]https://www.getapp.com/resources/decade-in-tech/

- Model the behaviors you want to see from your students when it comes to emails and phone calls over the weekend or late in the evening.

- If you build it, they will come. It just might take a bit for them to get there.

Taking Action

List three possible reasons why some starfish may not attend live lessons that are offered:

_____

_____

_____

Why is it important to offer choices to students when scheduling live lessons and office hours?

_____

_____

_____

What are the benefits of practicing your conferencing tool prior to jumping in feet first with students?

_____

_____

_____

_____

Where do you plan on working during the day and how will you ensure that you can separate yourself from your workspace when necessary?

_____

_____

_____

_____

LLC: Live-Lesson Creation

Developing and delivering engaging live lessons

Whether you plan to use a live lesson to cover new material, review previously covered information, or to provide additional academic support, they must be planned in advance, just like you would create your lesson plan for a new lesson you would present to students in a traditional classroom. It takes time to take what you did in a classroom setting and manipulate it to fit your new online world.

The good news is that every single lesson you have created for a F2F classroom can be adjusted to fit your new teaching environment. It may take time to wrap your brain around adjusting what you have into something that engages students in an online setting, but give it time, take baby steps, and be fearless! Try new things along the way. The worst thing that can happen is that it doesn't work out as planned, you learn from your experience, and you move forward more prepared for your next attempt.

Determining the Length of Your Live Lesson

Live-lesson time frames differ based on grade level but should not go longer than forty-five to sixty minutes **max,** including reflection time and opportunities to answer questions. This time frame will vary depending on the age of your students. Older students can handle longer sessions, while elementary and middle school students will benefit from having shorter online meetings.

Limiting Student Attendance

When you think about how many students to allow into the live lesson at once, first consider the limitations of any software you're using. Then, remember that best practice is to keep group sizes to a minimum. There is no magic number; however, keeping attendance under twenty participants will help, which may mean you need multiple sessions for each class.

At first, you might think it's smart to invite the masses and cram as many digital faces into one room as possible. But having a large group of students in a live lesson can make behavior management, meaningful conversation, and engagement a challenge.

You should consider inviting a colleague to join and act as your partner in crime if you plan on bringing in more than five students, unless you're a gambler like my late grandmother was (you couldn't drag her away from a slot machine). A coteacher can offer support such as responding to questions posed in the chat box. This will help you maintain a better handle on moderating the lesson and meeting each student's individual needs.

In addition to offering you support, partnering could also help your fellow educator learn new techniques and tools for offering live lessons of their own.

Live-Lesson Planning

Let's take a look at seven steps for live-lesson planning. Also, don't forget to check out the *Live-Lesson Checklists* found in the Resources section of the book.

Preplanning

Determine the lessons/content that you would like to connect with your live lesson. Consider the content students have most difficulty with interpreting and/or understanding.

Create a Learning Goal

Pinpoint what you want your students to be able to do at the end of your live lesson. For example: *Students will be able to explain verbally how to add double-digit numbers.* Your learning goal should be based on grade level standards or benchmarks.

Activate Prior Knowledge

Do your students have prior knowledge about the topic you will be covering and can provide a link to OR will you have to build background knowledge before digging into the learning goals? Consider using polls, pictures, videos, brainstorming, and word clouds to access prior knowledge to determine where your jumping-off point will be.

Plan Content Delivery

Take time to brainstorm and plan what you will use to deliver your content. This might include creating PowerPoint slides, showing a short video, placing students into small groups to create a product, or using online tools such as Nearpod or Kahoot to deliver content. Have fun with this and don't hold back on creativity. You can even consider coming up with a theme and dressing up to enhance engagement (something I've done before).

The author embracing the theme of a live lesson

Time for Engagement

One of the most important aspects of online content delivery is determining how students will interact with the information you share. In other words, what will the students do while they are in the lesson? This is the engagement piece and can make or break the effectiveness of your live lesson.

Many of the same best practices and planning tools that you may have used within the four physical walls of your classroom can be used in an online lesson. Think about using the structure of I DO, WE DO, YOU DO when planning activities for your online lessons.

Suggestions

- Create a note-taking guide for students to use and follow along.
- Give students opportunities to share thoughts and/or feelings with the group.
- Create an engaging activity using an app such as Nearpod.

- Use breakout rooms and have students create something on a shared document.
- Allow students to use drawing tools to illustrate a concept or practice a new skill.
- Show a video in place of lecturing about a topic for an extended period.

Check for Understanding

Just as you would in a brick-and-mortar classroom, you need to make sure your kiddos are following along and absorbing what you're teaching them. During the lesson, you might consider asking them to grab the mic to share their thoughts and findings with other students or to use the nonverbal communication tools to complete quick checks (more to come on these). You can also have them submit a reflection sheet as a follow-up activity or complete and submit an assignment for grading.

The key is to determine what evidence of learning you will collect to ensure that each student has mastered the concepts!

Follow-Up

Your next step is to decide how to follow up with those students who do not show mastery of the concept taught. It can be easy to let them go their separate ways and not follow up, but it's critical that we put practices in place to catch those students who need more instructional support.

Ways to follow up include pulling a small group of students together at another time, giving the student a phone call for some one-on-one instruction, or emailing the student additional resources or an enrichment activity.

Getting the Word Out

After you've planned your lesson, it's time to deliver it! It's important to let students know when a live lesson will be taking place well in advance. Just like us, students need time to plan for things.

You can market your session using any of the following ideas:

- Post information about the day and time on your course homepage "above the fold" so they don't have to scroll down far to see it.

- Send meeting information via email or text message the week before. Send a reminder as you get closer to the date and be sure to mention it during phone calls with students.

- Be creative with the title of your lesson. Students are much more likely to join in on a session named "True Earth Facts You Must See to Believe" than a session called "Tectonic Plates and Tides."

- When creating your PowerPoint presentation, consider using the rule of five: No more than **five** words per line of text, **five** lines of text per slide, or **five** text-heavy slides in a row.

> Practice starting your live lessons and office hours on time. During live lessons, give students a five-minute buffer when logging in. Beyond that, it is a life lesson to not allow students to attend if they are late or have missed a portion of the information being shared.

Starting the Lesson

Upon entering your live-lesson session, you need to set the stage and immediately grab students' attention. One way to do this is through music. I remember during tests when I taught in brick-and-mortar schools, I'd sometimes play opera as a way to get them to focus.

Next, provide students with something to do. For instance, have students sign into an online attendance sheet to get the ball rolling. This type of document can be created within Office 365 or Google Forms. Most often, students will want to socialize and say hello to each other in the chat box as others are logging in.

> **Live Lesson SEL**
>
> A good way to incorporate SEL in your live lesson is by doing a quick check-in at the start of the lesson. Ask the students how they are doing and tell them to use the available nonverbal chat icons to show how they are feeling that day. This will give you a good idea as to where each student is emotionally that day.
>
> 😊 ☹️ 😐
> Happy   Sad   Okay

Once you're ready to dive into your content, you may need to use a "mute all" button, if available, take away microphone privileges for your attendees, or give students an opportunity to quiet down before you begin.

Before you start digging into content, review "ground rules" or behavior expectations with students. Ground rules might include things such as:

- Be on time.
- Be aware of your surroundings. Check your background to make sure there aren't any unexpected surprises like Grandma walking by in her jammies.
- Be school appropriate and have respectful chatter related to the lesson being shared.
- Be kind to others and respect the thoughts and opinions of fellow students.
- Actively participate throughout the lesson.

Once ground rules are covered, it's a good idea to go over the tools that are offered in your online classroom. Things to review and have students practice might be:

- How to use the chat box
- How to turn their cameras on and off
- Where to find things such as nonverbal communicators often shown as a red X or green check
- How to use drawing or writing tools that might be used to have students write directly on the screen. This will not be necessary if you won't be using this type of tool during your lesson.
- How to save a copy of their screens if submitting for credit once the live lesson has wrapped up.

Engage, Don't Lecture

How many times were you in a meeting and talked at for an hour? And, during that time, did you ever successfully plan your entire shopping list, decide what dress you will wear out on Saturday, and remember where you put those misplaced keys? Of course, you have.

Engagement is key for online learning and talking at students is definitely not engaging them. So, when holding an online meeting or live lesson, you don't want to dominate the session. It's important to get the students involved in the conversation, otherwise they will tune you out. Need ideas for breaking up your discussion points? Try some of these suggestions:

- Ask questions along the way to check for understanding.

- Provide students with at least ten seconds of wait time between posing questions. This gives students the opportunity to think about how they want to respond before they do.

- Ask for feedback from participants by encouraging them to pick up the mic to share with others or use a chat box to respond, if available.

- Use any nonverbal communication tools provided with online conferencing program. These icons, like checkmarks, thumbs-down, thumbs-up, and a raised hand, give you interaction similar to walking around the perimeter of a brick-and-mortar room, scanning each student with your eyes to ensure they are following along.

If you find that several students are not responding, be sure you walk them through the how-tos of using the interactive conference tools available and repeat the directions a few times.

Refrain from calling students out by name if they are not responding to your requests. You never know what might be happening on the other end of that line, and if you embarrass a student during one of your meetings, in front of peers, you may never see that student online again. If you notice that a student is not responding to your questions or prompts to provide feedback, a best practice would be to make note of the student's name and reach out by phone after your online session.

Finally, remember that it will be difficult to fit everything you might want to share in a fifty-minute class period during an online session with your students. Not only will you be sharing information with your students, you'll also be checking for understanding throughout your session, monitoring student behavior, answering questions that students may have, working around possible internet and technical issues, and more. What you covered in your traditional classroom will need to be tweaked to fit your new virtual world.

> **Making the Most of the Chat Box**
>
> When it comes to student engagement, nonverbal communication tools can be your best friend. If your online meeting tool provides a thumbs-up, checkmark, or other icons, encourage your participants to use them! These icons are great ways to check in with your students throughout the session. At the start of the meeting, have them respond using an icon to confirm that they can hear you talking. This will help weed out students who might be having audio issues and you'll know who needs help. If following the best practice of having a co-teacher in your session, allow them to tackle those students who are having issues with audio or logging in while you move forward with the curriculum.
>
> Another way to use the chat box during your session is to ask questions that force students to respond with a checkmark or X to show understanding. If you're not checking in with your students throughout your session, you will easily become like yet another commercial break in their day and they will tune you out.

Handling Disruption and Behavior Issues

Some students will make poor choices and will be inappropriate during your meeting. Examples of this can include taking over the chat box with inappropriate language, drawing inappropriate body parts on the screen, and yelling over the mic. This is why it's so important to know your conferencing tool and how to use it effectively. Frankly, I don't think the MUTE ALL button gets the attention and accolades it deserves. Use this if it is available to you!

And if a student is out of control in a session, don't be afraid to remove them from the meeting altogether. Once your meeting/live lesson is over, take a deep breath and reach out to the student by phone to discuss behavior issues and what your expectations are for any upcoming meetings. Remember those life lessons we discussed before? This is one of them—hold students accountable for their actions.

After the Meeting

YOU DID IT! You completed your first live lesson! Now what? Take an opportunity to do something that we, as educators, often don't allow ourselves the time to do: self-reflect.
What went well? What can you improve for next time? What will you never do again? Once you feel up for it, ask a trusted coworker to come and observe a live lesson and provide you with specific feedback. This can be an opportunity for growth for everyone involved!

Not quite ready to offer your students a full-on live lesson? I understand! It takes time to adjust to teaching online and, in a perfect world, I wouldn't suggest any new online teacher hold a live lesson with students for at least your first month of teaching online. This is the time to get your feet wet, get comfortable with your new position, and work to understand the requirements of your new job. However, this is not often our reality, and you may find yourself being told to jump into the deep end of the pool.

If you feel like you want to see your students but aren't ready to create a full lesson for them, consider offering office hours and meeting with students individually in a virtual classroom setting.

Secrets of Success

- Set ground rules of behavior and academic expectations prior to starting any live lesson.

- Make sure if using PowerPoint slides that your slides are not too text heavy.

- Bullet information to cut down on paragraphs of reading on the page.

- Give plenty of wait time when asking students questions, counting to ten in your head, before moving on.

- Check in with students on a regular basis using your nonverbal communication icons.

- Keep your audience's age in mind when planning live lessons. Younger students' attention span will be shorter than students who are in high school or older.

- Consider having a follow-up activity/reflection sheet that they share with you once they have logged out to show what they learned during your time together.

- Not ready to offer a live lesson? Try providing office hours to get your feet wet!

Taking Action

What are two student behaviors seen during a live lesson that would show students are **actively engaged** in the information? What could it look like?

_____

_____

_____

_____

What are two student behaviors seen during a live lesson that would be signs of **disengagement**? What would it look like?

_____

_____

_____

_____

What are two strategies I can use to engage students during a live lesson?

_____

_____

_____

_____

What are some ways I can check for understanding during a live lesson?

_____

_____

_____

_____

What will my next step be if I find some students aren't grasping the information or concept I'm teaching during a live lesson?

_____

_____

_____

_____

How can I transfer the concept of a successfully delivered brick-and-mortar lesson into a live lesson?

_____

_____

_____

_____

What are three things I can do to market live lessons or office hours to students?

_____

_____

_____

_____

TGIF: Teaching and Guiding with Intentional Feedback

> *"In our virtual setting, feedback is our ultimate tool for differentiating student learning. It allows for us to provide our students with the instruction that they need, when they need it."*
>
> Former Pasco eSchool Teacher of the Year

Our online learners need timely, actionable, personalized feedback. It helps students grow and allows us to continue building the relationships we've nurtured from day one. More importantly, our feedback is something that students crave! In a recent survey conducted by an instructor at Pasco eSchool, 86 percent of student respondents reported that they ALWAYS read the feedback their teachers leave on assignments. Further, 81 percent reported that they wanted to be corrected more, because earning an "easy A" made them feel like their teacher didn't care.

We should give students feedback daily as part of our teaching. If we don't put the time and effort into providing our students with meaningful feedback, we are doing them a disservice and not taking advantage of the opportunities to teach, reteach, encourage growth, and support our students throughout their journeys in our virtual classrooms. One easy guideline to follow when you want to ensure valuable feedback is the STARR method.

Providing STARR Feedback

- **S**ay hello to your students by name. We build stronger teacher/student relationships when we address students by name. When we don't take the time to include the student's name, feedback can come across as being "canned" or impersonal. Of students surveyed in 2018 by a Pasco eSchools instructor about feedback, 51 percent said that having their name on feedback was really important, because it showed their teacher recognized them. Only 4 percent of students said seeing their name wasn't important at all.

- **T**ake the time to celebrate the positives. Letting our students know what they are doing *right* will help them understand what we want them to keep doing! It can be difficult at times to find the positives, I get it. Even just taking a moment to recognize that they're submitting an assignment for grading helps them see you are paying attention.

- **A**llow students to resubmit work to ensure mastery before moving forward. This is the beauty of working online. No longer are you tied to a bell schedule that dictates when you must move on to the next subject, topic, learning goal, benchmark, etc. Your students now have the opportunity to go back and review assignments that they didn't understand, have some one-on-one time with you, and then resubmit their assignment to prove they've mastered the concept!

- **R**eteach and provide academic feedback that is actionable, personalized, and promotes growth.

Providing our students with feedback gives us the opportunity to:

- Reteach information that students may not have mastered.
- Pose additional academic questions to solidify student learning.
- Provide students with additional resources when necessary.
- Challenge them to push themselves further in their understanding.

Feedback consisting of statements such as "Good job," "Well done," or "Please resubmit" is throwing away the potential for the most meaningful interaction you can have with online learners. Be sure to explain <u>why</u> something was good, <u>what</u> they did well, and what <u>action</u> they need to take prior to resubmitting their work.

- **R**emember to sign off on your student feedback with your name! Student feedback is all about personalization so each of your online learners feels like your only student. Be sure to include a closing each time you provide a student with academic feedback. It might be a little thing, but it makes a big difference.

Providing Timely Feedback

Not only do students want our feedback but they want it fast. In that report I mentioned earlier, 85 percent of student respondents said they wished they'd had access to their feedback earlier in the term so they could adjust their study habits and get help.

So, how fast is fast enough for feedback? Best practices for grading is to respond to student work within forty-eight hours or the same day when possible. If we wait for days or weeks to respond to a student's work, our feedback loses its power because they've moved on and it takes away from the learning continuity. Often, a student will hold off on submitting their next assignment until they receive a grade and feedback on the one most recently submitted. You can see where our lack of urgency could cause an issue when it comes to motivating students to move forward in a timely manner.

Feed Forward

Feed forward is a concept based on giving students a heads-up about what's coming next. Over time, you'll notice that some assignments become virtual roadblocks as students navigate through your course. These are the lessons that tend to slow them down, sometimes all the way to a complete stop.

When students hit a roadblock in a course, they can become frustrated or overwhelmed and will often walk away. By using the feed-forward strategy, you're giving students a heads-up as to what to expect on their next assignment so they are prepared for the challenge and up to the task.

Let's look at an example. In module three, lesson four of a course, students are asked to create a PowerPoint presentation that explains the phases of the moon. Students need to take pictures of the moon every two nights for two weeks and include those photos in their PowerPoint presentation. Over time, let's say you find yourself repeatedly providing feedback, asking students to go back to the lesson and provide the photos that they took over the course of two weeks. This leads to students having to resubmit the assignment, which, if we're being honest, leads to additional grading on your end.

If you were to use the feeding-forward strategy, you might add something like the following on the end of your feedback to assignment 3.4:

> Your next assignment gives you an opportunity to observe the phases of the moon! To earn full credit, you must submit eight to ten pictures of the moon within a PowerPoint presentation. Don't forget to include a drawing of one of the phases of the moon so that you can earn full credit on your assignment. I can't wait to see your hard work and effort come my way!

Efficiency Tips

It doesn't matter whether your curriculum was created for you or if you're writing your own lessons in your virtual classroom. It will take awhile to get efficient in responding to student assignments. It will be a process of getting familiar with the assignments and the expectations for each. It's important to be mentally prepared for this and to embrace the idea of feeling like you're moving at a snail's pace when initially working through your new online course and responding to student work.

There are some tried-and-true strategies that can be implemented that will help you to not only be efficient in your grading but also effective.

Save Your Grading/Feedback Notes

One of the most time-intensive parts of your day likely will be providing student feedback, and that's as it should be. This is your opportunity to guide your students toward success and clarify any confusion on their assignments. Here's the thing, though—there will be some assignments that end up requiring the same general response over and over ... and over.

For example, those assignments that are submitted with a missing required attachment. Your response to this might be something like, "Thank you so much for submitting this assignment for grading. However, it looks like your attachment didn't go through. Please try again for me!" Instead of typing this several times throughout the day, save this statement into a Word doc or other online tool such as OneNote. Then, when you receive another missing attachment, you can simply copy and paste this feedback into the assignment and return it to the student for another shot.

This strategy can be helpful for assignments that you respond to in similar ways based on the assessment requirements. When you save your general responses, and then personalize them to fit individual students' needs, it can save time on typing the same response over and over again.

Feedback

When saving your feedback to a Word doc or other tool, list your feedback in the same order as your course. Then, when you're grading, you won't find yourself scrolling through your saved feedback to find the one you're looking for.

For example:

Mod 1 lesson 1: Hello, [**insert student name here**], Thank you for attempting to submit your assignment on tectonic plates! The work you did was not attached to the message, however, so please resubmit so I can see the awesome job you did, and you can receive full credit! Mrs. Awesome Teacher

Mod 1 lesson 5: Hello, [**insert student name here**], Thank you for submitting your assignment for grading. You have done a nice job at X, Y, and Z. I like that you included A, B, and C in your work. Thank you for taking your time and submitting quality work. Mrs. Awesome Teacher

Mod 1 lesson 6: Hello, [**insert student name here**], Wow! You have done a fabulous job drawing a picture of the water cycle. Your definition of groundwater is spot on. In your next assignment, be sure to include a video to receive full credit. Mrs. Awesome Teacher

Group Grading

If your learning management system provides you with a way to sort assignments by individual lessons while grading student work, use this tool. This allows you to group like assignments together and provides you with an opportunity to grade several similar assignments, one after another, to get practice on what the grading requirements are before moving on to another assignment.

If you jump back and forth between assignments when grading multiple assignments at one time, this can cut down on your overall efficiency because it forces your brain to skip from one set of expectations to another.

Late Work and Cheating

Before we discuss how to deal with late work and cheating, I first want you to remember what we learned earlier in the book: Walk away when you're ticked off and assume everyone has the best intentions.

The truth is, we don't know what our kiddos could be dealing with on a day-to-day basis. No matter what happens, try not to take it personally when a student is late or cheats. Even when you have to discipline them, do so with both grace and empathy.

Late Work

In an online setting, "late" work doesn't always hold the same meaning as it might have in a brick-and-mortar setting. One of the benefits of an online class is that we have the ability to provide students with additional time to complete assignments and to go back and attempt assignments over again to master concepts. In my experience, students are allowed to resubmit work for additional grading right up to the point when they would be taking their final exam.

Additionally, keep in mind that you generally can't lower a student's grade on an assignment based on behavior. Failure to submit work on time is an unwanted behavior but shouldn't tie to academics. As always, check with your district/school's policies to see what the expectations are for grading late student work.

Cheating ... Oh No You Didn't!

As you work with your online learners and review their assignments, you'll get to know their writing styles and skill levels just as you would in a traditional setting. And, just like in a traditional brick-and-mortar classroom, there will be times when students try to pull one over on you. Yep. You will have students who try to cheat in your course.

In a traditional classroom, cheating might consist of writing answers down on the palm of their hand or leaning gently to the right to eyeball the paper of the person next to them. Or—and I may or may not have personal experience with this one—erasing your friend's name from her paper and writing your name larger and with darker glitter ink.

There are a variety of reasons why a student might choose to use the work of others or plagiarize from a friend or website. In some cases, students fail to realize that what they've done is a violation of academic integrity. Often, it's something as simple as them using information from a website or document without appropriately citing the source. However, I would be remiss if I didn't face the fact that students will sometimes choose to cheat to cut corners or out of academic anxiety due to pressures at home or from peers.

> **"Academic integrity (AI) means** acting with the values of honesty, trust, fairness, respect, and responsibility in learning, teaching, and research."[9]

As much as a discovery of cheating might make you want to jump in your car and show up at the cheater's doorstep, that would be frowned upon.

Unwritten rule #776 of online teaching states:

One shall not drive to a student's home to cry foul upon discovering evidence of cheating.

I am asking you to shift your perspective on academic integrity infractions from one of "cheater" to one of a "teachable moment." This can be difficult when we feel betrayed, disappointed, and annoyed. However, once you can remove yourself emotionally from the equation and embrace the opportunity to teach a life lesson, these situations will become less overwhelming. Remember, it's a bad choice and doesn't define who the student is as a person.

---

[9] Exemplary Academic Integrity Project (EAIP): Embedding and extending exemplary academic integrity policy and support frameworks across the higher education sector (2013), Plain English definition of Academic Integrity, Office for Learning and Teaching Strategic Commissioned Project 2012-2013, http: www.unisa.edu.au/EAIP.

So, what do you do? Here are some proven strategies that will help make these situations less stressful.

- When stumbling across integrity issues while grading student work, refrain from addressing it in writing. In your feedback, simply leave a note asking the student to give you a call to discuss the assignment. We should not be threatening, accusing, or pointing virtual fingers at anyone. Remember what you learned about email tone in the CSI chapter. This isn't a crime scene, and you aren't Sherlock.

- Double-check to be sure any reported matches do not include the actual questions from the assignment itself. If your school uses a built-in system that scans student work for plagiarism, it might not be trained to recognize when a student has copied and pasted questions into a document and will often tag them as a direct match to another assignment that has been submitted.

- Make a note in your schedule to follow up with the student in two to three days to give an opportunity for the student to check your feedback.

- If the student doesn't reach out to you by phone, email, or text within a couple days, give the student and parents a call! Although this call is about a serious concern regarding academics, the ten-second rule still holds true. Always, always, always ask them how they are doing. Jumping in and starting off with a conversation about a possible AI incident won't do you any favors when it comes to starting the call on the right foot. These phone calls can be uncomfortable for everyone involved and even if they are guilty of AI, the student still deserves our care.

- Once you confirm that all is well, here is one way you can rip off the bandaid and move forward: "Do you have any idea why I might be calling you about lesson 3.03?"

This type of open-ended questioning allows students an opportunity to fess up and come clean. Some will grasp hold of this get-out-of-jail-free card and verbally vomit all over you. Others will stand their ground and not budge. Sometimes, this is truly because they don't understand that what they have done is an issue; so, in their heads, they have nothing to admit.

If your student shares that they used a friend's work, copied from a website, or paid someone else to do the work, this is your moment to shine! This is where you can use your stellar customer-service skills and ask questions such as:

- Is there something going on that made you choose to do this?
- Are you not understanding the course material?
- Next time, what can you do if you don't understand something in class?

Be sure to share your conversation with the student's parents, too, so that you're all on the same page and have a clear understanding about how to avoid the same situation in the future. This would also be a good time to discuss the consequences of such choices and any follow-up activities that the student may need to complete. Refer to the CSI chapter if you find yourself in a situation with an upset parent on the other end of the line.

Once you have the full story, you'll most likely need to follow through with the policies and procedures your distinct has put into place for this type of behavior. Be sure to reach out and clarify your next steps.

> If your LMS does not have an integrated plagiarism checker, you can highlight text that is submitted to you online, right click, and select "Search with Google" to see where the text might match to similar text online.

Secrets of Success

- Follow the STARR method when providing academic feedback.

- Provide students with a heads-up on upcoming assignments by using the feeding-forward strategy.

- Clump like assignments together when grading student work.

- Save a copy of standard feedback that you find yourself typing over and over again. Then copy, paste, and personalize while grading student work!

- Steer clear of mentioning academic integrity issues in student feedback or within emails.

- Possible cheating = teachable moment.

Taking Action

When providing a student with academic feedback, it is important that I include the following components:

_____

_____

_____

_____

How can I feed forward in the future to cut down on confusion and virtual roadblocks?

_____

_____

_____

_____

Two efficiency strategies that I will give a try when grading student work are:

_____

_____

_____

_____

Practice incorporating STARR feedback in the example below:

Lesson directions:
2.04 Draw a picture of the water cycle, making sure to include and label the following parts of the system in your creation:

- *Groundwater*
- *Precipitation*
- *Condensation*
- *Infiltration*
- *One example of a watershed*
- *Evaporation*

Your student Sara submits the following work drawing as an attachment to her assignment:

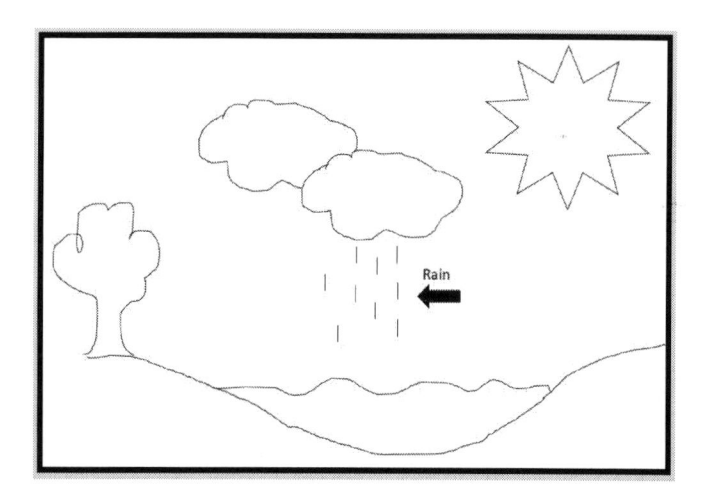

Practice providing STARR feedback in response to the example on the prior page. Base your feedback on the lesson requirements and work that was submitted.

_____

_____

_____

_____

When I come across a situation where a student has plagiarized or copied from a friend, I will take the following steps:

_____

_____

_____

_____

TMI: Time Management Ideas

"What smells? Oh ... that's me."
The importance of following a schedule!

Teachers are managers. They manage a classroom, they manage a course load, they manage information delivery—most of all, they manage time. Or, well, they *should* manage time.

If you're trying to handle virtual instruction like a game of whack-a-mole, simply bashing tasks in the head as they come at you rather than having a defined schedule for tasks, you're going to tire quickly, and worse, you're probably going to lose the game.

Schedules are like diets. You've got to stick with them to see results, and when you do, you'll wake up to a whole new you. This is one of the hardest parts of forcing yourself to follow a schedule. If you're like me, you might have a tendency to stop doing things if you don't see immediate results. But be patient! It may take a few weeks of dedicated schedule following for you to see the difference.

Following a schedule will help give you a sense of accomplishment. It will show you that you *are* making headway, even when it might not feel like you've done a single thing.

Right On Schedule

Again, much like diets, when it comes to scheduling, what works for one person may not work for another. The examples found here are simply meant to get you started. Some of them are the tried-and-true schedule other teachers have followed for years. My schedule, on the other hand, changes monthly ... sometimes weekly. Don't be afraid to adapt your schedule to fit *your* needs. A coworker might swear by the one that they have shared with you, but don't feel like you have to keep it as is. I don't want to see you dragging stuffed animals out on a leash just because a schedule here tells you to walk the dog at 10 a.m.

That leads me to my next point. Don't create your schedule and then print out fifty-two copies of it for each week of the year. Remember, your schedule can and will change along the way to meet your needs. At least fifty copies of that printed schedule will become scratchy toilet paper. Print one to two weeks at a time to save your sanity, trees, and your bottom.

Allowing for Flexibility

Life is unpredictable. Despite your best efforts at planning, there will be days when your kiddo is at home sick, days when you're sick, and days when your fur baby is throwing up all the things he ate yesterday. Yes! Life happens and can throw us off track. It's important to have flexibility in our day for when the unexpected occurs.

If something doesn't get done on Monday, the beauty of being in charge of your own day is that you can scoot it right over to Tuesday's to-do list. You won't want to do this too often, however, or you'll end up with a poop storm of a Friday.

Take advantage of downtime. There are certain times of the school year when your workload is lighter. Fewer meetings, less work being submitted, fewer phone calls, just plain less work. There will be other times when you'll be struggling just to keep your head above water, while once again contemplating whether you can survive off of Starbucks' wages.

These times will ebb and flow throughout the year, and with some experience under your belt, you'll adapt to these cycles, learn what to expect, and develop tools and strategies for making it through the more challenging times. In an upcoming chapter, you will be asked to come up with a plan B for when things don't go the way you planned. Start giving that some thought now (look at that feeding forward I just did!).

To truly be successful in an online setting, it's important to release the idea that any day is going to go exactly as planned. Embrace the crazy. There will be days where you start off ready to rule the world, only to be sidetracked by unexpected emails, lengthy phone calls, removal of objects from various child orifices, and so on. Allow for flexibility to adjust to what each workday throws your way, much like a chameleon adjusting to its surroundings. If you find yourself struggling to get on task, consider trying one of these tips:

- Work somewhere other than inside your home. A friend's house, a restaurant, coffee shop, or even a park can give you a break from day-to-day home stressors. Just make sure your young kids have adult supervision while you're gone. I don't want to see you on the news later.

- Use apps to monitor how you spend your time while working from home. There are a variety of free apps available that will help in tracking the amount of time you spend working throughout the day and the amount of time spent on a specific task. These can be helpful to those of us who find ourselves being sucked into the black hole of time while working online. Check out Focus Keeper!

- Try the Pomodoro Technique. This is a strategy in which you set a timer and work for an interval of time (say twenty-five minutes), then you break for a short interval (such as five minutes). It's much easier to focus on tasks, especially dreaded ones, when you know that you only have to do so in twenty-five-minute chunks that precede a reward of a five-minute Facebook/Insta scroll.

- Create a routine. Sometimes you need a physical way to get you into a deep work groove. Maybe that means grabbing your favorite pen and steno pad. Maybe it means putting on some reading glasses and throwing your hair up in a messy bun. My best friend and I use the saying "curl up." It means to get comfortable, grab a coffee, and focus. We use this when we need to clear out everything else in the world and home in on the tasks in front of us.

> Remember way back in the WTF chapter, we discussed adding a category in your schedule for browsing your *Things To Do* email folder and a check-off line to ensure you don't overlook tasks? Time to get that done!

Schedule Time for You

Ask yourself the following question: When was the last time I showered?

If it took you longer than four seconds to answer that question, I have news for you—it's been too long. That smell that's been following you around, the one you've been blaming on the cat? Um ... let's just say you owe Fluffy an apology.

Here's the good news: your stinkiness shows that you are ALL IN and have really jumped in with both unwashed feet. You should be so proud of yourself! But, now it's time to get in the shower and adjust your daily schedule. If you don't do it for yourself, do it for the others who have to live with you!

Your schedule needs to include time for you. Showering, eating three meals a day, taking part in fun activities like spending time with family, reading, exercise, gardening, playing tennis—you have to make time for these things. If you don't, you'll start to resent the fact that you're spending so much time online and burn out will be right around the corner.

Don't feel guilty for taking care of you and making sure that your needs are met. Your work will always be there waiting for you.

Schedule Examples

Here are a variety of schedules you can try. Remember, your schedule is *yours*. Use these examples to get started, but don't be afraid to change course and personalize them for your needs.

Chunking Schedule

Divide responsibilities into morning, afternoon, and evening blocks—not super time sensitive, but more of a general time frame or flow for your day to get things done. This is for those of us who are looking for flexibility in their day and don't thrive off strict guidelines.

- Morning: grade work, appointment calls
- Afternoon: outgoing calls, respond to emails
- Evening: grade student work, respond to missed phone calls

Hourly Schedule

This one is perfect for the type-A personality who likes to know what is coming next and have the day planned out in specific time frames with a detailed task list.

- 9 a.m.–10 a.m.
    - Monthly call appointments
    - Welcome call appointments
    - Call students who haven't worked in 10–14 days
- 10 a.m.–12 p.m.
    - Grade student work
    - Go for a walk
- 12 p.m.–1 p.m.: Lunch
- 1 p.m.–3 p.m.
    - Return missed calls and respond to emails
- 4 p.m.–6 p.m.
    - Student appointments
    - Grade student work
    - Respond to emails

Daily Check-Off Schedule

This is a list of items that need to be done before the computer is shut down at the end of the day. They're not time bound other than getting them done before the end of the workday.

Monday:
____ Send weekly update. Include reminders for this week's live sessions or office hours, tips of the day, work expectations, what you did over the weekend, anything you want students/parents to know.
____ Grade student work (turn off phone/emails during this time—remember that you can use the Do Not Disturb option on email and phone to cut down on distractions).
____ Check/reply to email
____ Return any missed calls

Tuesday:
____ Check/reply to email
____ Grade student work
____ Return missed calls
____ Contact next group of 25 students for monthly phone call
____ Send email/text message reminder to students regarding live lessons

Making Time for Professional Development

It's important to make time for professional development and learning from others who have done this job. But at the start of your journey, it may not be the best time to sign up to take a million online classes or PD sessions. Get your footing and the basics down and wait until you feel more comfortable before adding more to your plate.

You will probably be going through some sort of training the first few weeks of transitioning online. It might be formal training where you have a mentor, instructional coach, or seasoned online teacher guiding you through your first few weeks of your new adventure. Anything in addition to your basic job functions and needs should be put aside for now. Not forever, just for now.

The learning curve when jumping into the online world is steep. It's NOT a time to be worried with additional professional development activities.

Try to hold off on taking on additional responsibilities until you acclimate to your new position. That means STOP SAYING YES to every freaking thing! It's okay to step back and learn your new position. You'll be able to jump right back in, taking on too much stuff and regretting it later, in no time at all. Rock-star teachers will always have opportunities to do more, right?!

Secrets of Success

- Understand that your schedule will ebb and flow based on the time of year.

- Maintain flexibility with your schedule when things don't go as planned.

- Allow time during your day to practice self-care.

- When possible, turn down extra responsibilities during the first few months of your new position so you can focus on developing your new craft.

Taking Action

The type of schedule that I think would best fit my needs and personality would be the:
- ❏ Chunking schedule
- ❏ Hourly schedule
- ❏ Daily check-off schedule

Some daily teaching and personal responsibilities I would need to include in my work schedule are:

_____

_____

_____

_____

Sketch out the type of schedule you chose with the items that you have listed above.

_____

_____

_____

_____

BFF: Balancing Function and Family

"I love my family, but why won't they leave me alone?"
Tips and tricks for working at home

I remember the day I was hired to teach online from home. My husband and I were so excited that I would be able to stay home with our infant child while still managing to hold a full-time teaching position. It was like a dream come true ... until it wasn't.

I always heard that online teaching was awesome for those who had littles at home because you could be a stay-at-home mom while continuing your career. For me, working helped give me an identity beyond being a mom. Don't get me wrong—being a mom is awesome, but I wanted something that was mine, in addition to raising a family. It is important to me to teach my students **and** have the ability to be home with our children.

What I didn't understand was my online teaching gig was not just about me and my identity. It would turn out to be so much more than that. It would turn out to be an experience my entire family had to adjust to and embrace just as much as I did. It would be more challenging than my most challenging day in a brick-and-mortar classroom and more rewarding than I had ever imagined.

They Don't Always Get It

If I had an Oreo for every time one of my extended family members asked me what I did and how I could teach students over a computer, my blood would be nothing but cookie crumbs. "How can they learn like that?" "How do you know they're there if you can't see them?" "Are you sad that you left your REAL teaching job?" (This one makes me want to straight-up throat punch someone.)

No matter how many times I have tried to explain what I do, they just don't get it. It's not their fault. It's a foreign concept to many and just in the last fifteen years has really taken off. People, including my own friends and family, are skeptical of what it is, how it's done, and whether it's a real job. Don't try to get everyone to understand. It won't happen. Just tell them enough to get by: "I work from home. I work with students over the computer and they work on their computer from home. It's awesome! Now, please excuse me as I need to change my sweatpants for today's workday."

Because they often don't understand what you do or appreciate how time consuming it is, some family, friends, and even neighbors might see you as always being available for a chat, an errand, or a favor. This is something you need to nip in the bud immediately. Just cut that baby flower right off its stem. How? By setting boundaries whenever possible.

Let them know what your workweek looks like ahead of time so that they are aware of any meetings you might have. Set your cell phone to silent when in meetings so that unexpected calls don't distract you from your work responsibilities. Ask friends and family to wait until after a certain time of day to call. Let family and friend calls go to voicemail if they can't catch a hint. It will be okay—you can call them back. Or, respond via text letting them know you are currently in a meeting and unable to respond. It will take some training, but over time, MOST will get used to you working from home and start to respect your work hours.

Lord of the Phones

Whenever you are on the phone, expect for things to go wrong and expect to be interrupted. Look—it's even unwritten rule #181 of online teaching:

One shall expect both interruptions and disasters as soon as one engages in a phone conversation.

Maybe you've already experienced this and thought it was just you. Rest assured, it's not. I am certain that, when working from home, a phone conversation sends a signal to everyone around you that the competition for your attention has begun. It's like they have a secret meeting where they were briefed on this strategy. This will be the time that all humans shorter than four feet tall will need to pee, want a snack, spill a drink, flush something random down the toilet, let your inside cat of ten years outside while a wild pack of dogs are running by, cut their hair with your crafting scissors, stick random objects up their noses, use Sharpies to paint their nails ... the list goes on and on.

This is also the time that everyone in your home will ask you for food. Why? Because they know that the chances of you saying yes increased 110 percent as soon as you need them to leave you alone. Accept this now and be ready to adjust accordingly.

Here are some suggestions that might help:

- Make phone calls when younger kiddos are down for a nap or in bed.

- Plan an activity to occupy your children prior to jumping on the phone to make a call.

- Hide in the bathroom or a small closet if children are safe and you just need a quiet place.

- Be honest and real by letting your students know you have children at home with you. There's nothing wrong with sharing this information and it makes you more real. It helps for them to think of you as more than just a computer and more of a human being. However, if you have a screaming baby in the background or on your shoulder during every phone call and it becomes distracting, it's important to keep professionalism in mind. When it becomes distracting to our students, it can become a problem.

- If you're in a bind and have a little one at home with you during your workday, and they are cranky during a phone call, ask your student if the background noise is distracting and, if so, call them back in a few minutes when things have settled.

- Keep healthy snacks around for those moments of weakness when your children are pulling on your pant leg for their fifth snack of the day. Set up a bowl for each child, labeled with their name, and fill them with snacks that are readily available to them throughout the day. Once the snacks are gone, there is no more snacking.

- Take time out to eat lunch. Scheduling time to have lunch with your family will cut down on a lot of the harassing that can happen throughout the day due to hunger. I know this sounds ridiculous, right? But it's easy to get caught up in all the things you have going on in a day and forget to eat ... and subsequently lose track of time and not realize that little Johnny ate breakfast five hours ago and has turned to eating old crackers from between the couch cushions.

The Family Team

The most important lesson for you to take from this chapter is that teaching online is a team effort and your family is part of that team. Discuss with your family how they need to see themselves as an extended part of your team and what "positions" they play. If you don't, it will be a constant uphill battle. They have to respect the fact that you will need some time to hide away to be on the phone, to focus on grading student work, and that they need to be flexible during the times where you might be working extended hours. Most importantly, they need to see your work as **work**—even if to an outsider it looks like sitting in PJs on the couch with a laptop.

Before accepting an online teaching position, I suggest having a true heart-to-heart with your significant other. The idea of working from home can be glorious, but the reality is you are **working** from home and will need everyone to work together to make it successful.

During the early days of my online teaching career, my husband would take the baby from 6 to 8 p.m. every night in order for me to have phone time. He also would often cook dinner for our family. You have to figure out how to share duties in a way that works best for your family.

And you shouldn't feel guilty about needing the help of your teammates. I used to feel guilty, as if my working from home meant that all the dishes should be done, the clothes should be washed and folded, and the house should be spotless. The truth is, the house looks much the same as it would if I worked at a brick-and-mortar school for eight hours a day because, despite the location, I am still working eight hours a day. In addition, I'm working from home, so I'm actually making a mess at home when I'd otherwise be trashing up the teacher's lounge.

When your career is a true team effort, you have to be okay with letting some of that go and acknowledging that you are doing the best you can.

And despite your best intentions of being a stay-at-home parent and professional, that might not be possible for you. It wasn't for me. The original plan was to stay home and teach online so that I could keep my kiddos at home with me. I had visions of spending quality time with them between phone calls, eating picnic lunches in the park, singing nursery rhymes throughout the day, and snuggling right alongside them at nap time. Instead, I found myself flinging Goldfish crackers and chicken nuggets at them midday, occasionally having to gingerly pluck said crackers from their nostrils, and hiding in the closet to answer phone calls while trying to hold back my tears. I would rush them off to nap, crossing my fingers they would sleep longer today so that I could squeeze in just a few more calls.

Of course I love my family and I wanted to spend time with them. However, I also have a job. You know, one that I get paid to do each day? The one that helps pay the bills in our house and kinda needs my attention?

Along the way, I learned that scheduling blocks of time throughout the day to step away from the computer and sit and eat those lint-covered Goldfish crackers with my kiddos was important to all of us. Those moments gave me a mental break I probably wouldn't have taken otherwise, and precious moments to connect with my littles. These interim pauses reminded me that not every waking moment had to be spent pounding on computer keys.

As the kids grew older, we realized that our plans needed to change. The day my husband and I decided to put our oldest into preschool was the worst and best day of my life. He was only there for three hours a day, three days a week, but what a life-changing event that was for all of us.

I finally had some uninterrupted time to make calls, answer emails, focus on one thing. And you know, the focus I could have in a three-hour period was amazing. This protected time three days a week allowed me to enjoy the moments that he was home more because I wasn't so frantic and filled with anxiety trying to get things done with him there.

It's a huge decision to put a child in daycare, and I am not saying it's something every online teacher must do. Whatever choice you make for your family, I understand and respect. The point is, be open to making care arrangements if you can't find any other solution. If you're thinking about placing your child in care but are feeling nervous about doing so (much like I was), here are some suggestions.

- Find a trusted coworker who teaches for the same school as you or a friend who has children, too, and do a kid swap on certain days of the week. On the days where you take on an extra little person, be sure not to schedule meetings or many phone calls. This will help free up at least one day a week during which you can make uninterrupted phone calls while your child is at another teacher's home.

- Ask a trusted relative to take the kiddos on a consistent day every week for one hour. That's not asking very much but also gives you some reliable weekly alone time to focus on tasks that need undivided attention.

- Look for a preschool that offers two- or three-day schedules with shortened hours instead of a full five-day schedule. You'd be shocked at how much you can accomplish in just a few short hours when you have silence and can focus on one single thought at a time.

- When your child gets older, find places you can go that will keep them busy while you borrow the internet to work on grading or phone calls. Trampoline establishments are some of my favorite hangouts. Let them jump their hearts out while you sit on the sidelines using the Wi-Fi and drinking cheap coffee! WIN-WIN!

No matter what arrangements you make, you also need to have a plan B—that plan you put into place when something unexpected comes up. A sick child at home, for instance. How will you handle this when you are now working at home with little to no separation from family stress or unexpected circumstances? Is there a family member who you can reach out to for extra support during these times? Do you have the ability to call in sick for the day? Can your significant other take over for the day while you continue on as normal?

Remember, It Gets Better!

It'll take time for your family to adjust to your new adventure. Little ones will be so excited to have you home with them all day, they may forget you're actually working during this time (so might your spouse, parents, siblings, neighbors, and friends). Create a schedule and set boundaries—and stick to them. Things will get better over time, and you'll find it well worth the challenges.

On the flip side, I wouldn't do you any favors if I failed to mention that sometimes teaching online is not meant for everyone, and that's okay! Just like anything else in life, if you aren't willing to give it a shot, you'll never know if you really like it.

There's something to be said for standing up in front of a room full of kiddos and seeing their smiling faces each and every day. If you find that's where you belong, feel good that you tried something new and learned skills along the way, and be confident that you've found your true calling.

Otherwise, hang on for a wild ride! Are you ready?

Secrets of Success

- Recognize that certain family members and friends will NEVER fully understand what you do.
- Understand that this is a family affair.
- Give your family grace to adjust to the new norm.
- Use a Do Not Disturb sign on your office door if/when possible (one has been provided for you in the Resources area of this book).

Taking Action

Where do I see that challenges may arise with friends/family when working online from home?

_____

_____

_____

_____

How can I overcome those challenges?

_____

_____

_____

_____

What is my plan B?

_____

_____

_____

_____

When I think about teaching online, I get most excited about:

_____

_____

_____

_____

Conclusion

Inside this book are all—well, almost all—the things I wish I'd known when I first entered the virtual education space. With these best practices, tools, resources, and strategies, you can spend more time focused on the reason you became a teacher: to develop relationships with students and build a safe classroom with a strong sense of community.

And this is the main crux of why I wrote this book. For so many students, their time in school offers them an environment that they don't otherwise have. It gives them time to hope, time to feel safe, time to feel protected, and time to feel understood.

When I was growing up, school was often my safe place—a reprieve from the chaotic and emotionally damaging home in which I grew up. Today, hundreds or thousands of our students see school the same way I did.

As virtual teachers, we must do everything in our power to offer students the same sanctuary that brick-and-mortar schools offer. We should have enough mental and emotional resources to make our students feel safe, seen, respected, and confident. It is our collective responsibility to do so.

And that leads me to one major point that I wish someone would have shared with me before I made the switch to virtual teaching. When you can manage your time, rely on the right tools, and integrate the right processes, you free up so much more time and energy to build deeper, more meaningful relationships with your students and their families. Over the years, I can't tell you how many hours I've spent talking to students about—not schoolwork—but their *lives*. About their emotions. About the struggles they were facing.

Every moment that I've spent as a virtual instructor has offered me emotional rewards I never could have anticipated, and I'm so excited to see you embark on this same journey.

At the beginning of the book, I asked you about some of the distance-learning factors you were excited about, fearful of, and questioning. Let's see how you feel answering these same questions now.

What are the answers to the two questions you originally had about distance-learning and teaching students online?

_____

_____

_____

_____

What questions do you still have?

_____

_____

_____

_____

What did you gain by reading this book?

_____

_____

_____

_____

Are you still excited about the same thing? Have you added anything new that you're excited about?

_____

_____

_____

_____

Do you feel better equipped to deal with anything you listed as making you apprehensive/fearful about teaching online?

_____

_____

_____

_____

Now that you've read the book, what are some pros and cons you expect to encounter as you begin teaching online? How has this changed from your original list?

Pros:

_____

_____

_____

_____

Cons:

_____

_____

_____

_____

There's one last thought I'd like to leave you with. On this journey, you only get as much as you give. So, give your all to your kiddos. They deserve it—and so do you.

Resources

Lesson Planning Sheet

Preplanning: Topic to cover

_____

Learning goal: What they will be able to do?

_____

_____

_____

Activating prior knowledge: How I will activate their prior knowledge or build knowledge?

_____

_____

_____

_____

Activity: How I will deliver my information?

_____

_____

_____

_____

Check for understanding: How will I check to ensure they understand the learning goal?

_____

_____

_____

_____

Follow-up: What will I do if a student does not show mastery of a concept?

_____

_____

_____

_____

Live-Lesson Checklists

Prior to your live lesson:

- ❏ Market your live lessons like your life depends on it!

- ❏ Vary the times of day that you offer your lessons/office hours for those who might have challenging circumstances at home or scheduling conflicts.

- ❏ Less is more: Plan lessons that will last less than forty-five minutes, including time for questions.

- ❏ Always check your background before turning on your camera!

NOTES:

_____

_____

_____

_____

During your live lesson:

- ❏ Put yourself on screen to help bridge the gap of distance. Make sure to wear a nice shirt!

- ❏ Use a high-quality microphone and camera.

- ❏ Encourage your online learners to use the microphone and put themselves on camera, when appropriate.

- ❏ Provide time at the start of the meeting for an audio check.

- ❏ Go over behavior ground rules prior to starting your live lesson/online meeting.

- ❏ Check in frequently with students during lessons to monitor understanding and close gaps where needed.

- ❏ Provide students with a follow-up lesson to submit for grading to check for understanding.

NOTES:

_____

_____

_____

_____

Wrapping it up:

- ❏ Don't be discouraged when/if you have a low number of participants show up. Remember, it will take time!

- ❏ Give yourself a pat on the back for taking the leap and trying something new!

- ❏ Follow up with grading work that was submitted in response to attending your live lesson.

- ❏ Watch your recording to encourage personal and professional growth.

- ❏ Reflect on how your live lesson went! What went well? What can be improved for next time?

NOTES:

_____

_____

_____

_____

DO NOT DISTURB

That means YOU!

**In a meeting!
Shhhhhhhh**

About the Author

Desiré Mosser earned her bachelor of science degree in science education from Florida State University. After graduation, she taught middle grades science for six years before making the transition into virtual education.

Desiré worked with Florida Virtual School (FLVS) for eight years, first as a high school-level Earth Space Science teacher, then teaching a Leadership Skills Development course and eventually becoming a lead instructor. In this role, she supported a group of teachers by coaching them in best practices for online instruction.

While at FLVS, Desiré received the Marybeth Atwill Award for mentoring online instructors. She was her schoolhouse's Teacher of the Year for three consecutive years. In 2013 Desiré began working with Pasco eSchool as their instructional coach.

During her time with Pasco, she has supported a full eSchool staff of over 110 full-time instructors. She works to help teachers achieve success with their students, support professional development, and develop policies and procedures with the administration. Desiré also helped to create a blended-learning cohort to support all blended classrooms throughout Pasco County. In 2015 she was given the 2015–16 Pasco eSchool Teacher of the Year award.

Desiré presents at state conferences for virtual learning, providing valuable techniques to engage and motivate students. These presentations include Future of Education Technology Conference (FETC), the Florida Network of District Virtual Instructional Programs Symposium (FLDVIPN), and International Association for K-12 Online

Learning (iNACOL). She is also the creator of The Virtual Balcony Facebook page, providing motivation and encouragement to virtual teachers all over the world.

Author Contact Information

Email: MosserMotivates@gmail.com
Website: Desiremosser.com
Facebook: Facebook.com/The-Virtual-Balcony

SOS: Strategies for Online Survival

Made in the USA
Columbia, SC
02 September 2020